India-Mongolia Relations:
Beyond Greater Central Asia

India-Mongolia Relations:
Beyond Greater Central Asia

Editors

Sureyya Yigit

R Srinivasan

HOW
ACADEM/CS
an imprint of Highlyy Publishing LLP

in association with

PRAGHNA CENTRE FOR RESEARCH. TOWARDS A KNOWLEDGE DRIVEN SOCIETY.
PRAGHNA

ISBN: 978-93-95522-02-1 (Hardbound)
First Published : 2023

Cataloging in Publication Data--DK
Courtesy: D.K. Agencies (P) Ltd. <docinfo@dkagencies.com>
Webinar on India-Mongolia Relations: Beyond Greater Central Asia (2021 : Online)
India-Mongolia relations : beyond greater Central Asia / editors, Dr R Srinivasan, Prof. Sureyya Yigit.
pages cm
"This volume is a collation of the papers presented during the webinar on India-Mongolia Relations: Beyond Greater Central Asia held in July 2021"--Editor's note.
"... New Vision University, Georgia, and Praghna Centre for Research, Coimbatore, India, came together to host a webinar ..."--Preface.
ISBN 9789395522021 (Indian edition)
ISBN 9789395522069 (International edition)
1. India--Foreign relations--Mongolia--Congresses. 2. Mongolia--Foreign relations--India--Congresses. 3. Geopolitics--Asia, Central--Congresses. I. Srinivasan, R., 1961- editor. II. Yigit, Sureyya, editor. III. New Vision University (Tbilisi, Georgia), organizer. IV. Praghna Centre for Research (Coimbatore, India), organizer. V. Title.
LCC DS450.M65I53 2021 | DDC 327.5405173 23

Published by : HOW ACADEMICS
an imprint of Highlyy Publishing LLP

Correspondence Address : 4/30 A II Floor, Double Storey Buildings
Vijay Nagar, Delhi-110009
Editorial: +91 9811026449
Sales : +91 9999953412
Email: info@howacademics.com
Website: www.howacademics.com

Printed in India

Contents

Foreword

Ambassador Anil Trigunayat, IFS (Retd)

Special Address

Excellences, distinguished Speakers, dear friends,

I am indeed most grateful to my friend Dr R Srinivasan, Editor-in-Chief, Electronic Journal of Social and Strategic Studies, India and Professor Sureyya Yigit, New Vision University, Georgia, for organising this very important interaction about a country I really hold dear and where Indians are liked the most in the world. Reason was and remains historic and religious connect with Buddhism and being an integral part of larger Asia.

As for Georgia being the initiator of this conference allow me to add that we recently had the Indian Foreign minister Dr S Jaishankar visiting and handing over some of the remains, holy relics and artefacts of 17th Century St. Queen Ketevan of Georgia to the Government and people of Georgia reviving Georgia's "Goa Connect". He also unveiled the newly installed statue of Mahatma Gandhi in the city of Tbilisi.

I would like to extend my heartiest felicitations to my Mongolian friends for electing a new President a well-known politician whom I met in Moscow. Congratulations to HE. Ukhnaagiin Khurelsukh on his election as President of Mongolia.

As we have illustrious speakers analysing nearly every strategic dimension of Mongolia's external relation including with India, I would like to share only some of my personal experiences. I was posted as Deputy Ambassador to Mongolia during the most momentous period (1990-92) in its history when with the Soviet Union's disintegration Mongolia achieved a non-violent transition to democracy. The memories of clarion call for democracy and quiet protests are fresh even after three decades - when in -30 to -40 sub-zero temperatures people formed the human chains and the communist party led government conceded.

Historians have spoken about migration of some tribes from Kangra kingdom to Mongolian territory 4300 years ago. Mangaldev, son of the King headed the migrants and majority of them returned to India after staying there for about 2000 years though there is no historical evidence yet to prove this. In 1924, the then Prime Minister of Mongolia Mr. A. Amar mentioned in his book – "Short History of Mongolia" that Mongolian forefathers came from backside of Himalayan Mountains. Another interesting thing often quoted, is about 'Ganga Nuur' lake which according to many Mongolians derived its name after 'Ganga River' in India from where some Mongolian Lamas brought water and poured into the lake in Sukhbaatar Province and naming it so.

It is often said that the 3 Ds Democracy, Dharma and Development Partnership have emerged as the pillars of India Mongolia relationship.

I was in Mongolia during a very momentous period when Mongolia was trying to embrace democracy and get out of the Soviet era influence. Therefore, I was fortunate to have seen and witnessed the exceptional and indomitable spirit of our Mongolian brothers and sisters who fought for their rights and their hopes. Rest is history. Living through history for a diplomat is a highly rewarding experience as it also provides an opportunity to do something more for the people in that particular country. Mongolia was no exception for us.

I remember when I opted to go to Mongolia from Bangladesh my Ambassador, who later rose to be the Foreign Secretary, questioned my judgment. But apart from my exotic ideas about this beautiful land which generally was shrouded in mystery I was curious to work under the new ambassador Rinpoche venerable Kushok Bakula. It was indeed a most amazing experience a diplomat can possibly ask for. While Mongolia was going through the transition, they needed the symbols of love and religious beliefs and practices and that is the reason that Ambassador Bakula was loved by the Mongolians virtually as a living God. I remember we used to have miles long queues in front of our embassy for his darshans. What we achieved by that was further strengthening the bonds of love, tradition, Buddhism, history and civilization for which the contributions of Ambassador Bakula who revived large number of monasteries are simply stupendous. I also remember that whenever we sought an appointment with any of the leaders at the time, they were more than happy to enjoy the blessed company and the masterful diplomatic interaction with the ambassador. It provided us a tremendous P to P advantage. I remember the American and the British ambassadors often commenting that India had done a coup in Mongolia.

Let me talk a little more about this one man from my own experience – a saint and an Ambassador who cemented and etched India into the sub -conscious of every Mongolian and the people he came in contact with. This had a permanence that was unimaginable to many. His exceptional style of implicit soft power projection provided India a very unique and lasting impact.

I had read that over a century ago it was prophesied that Arhat Bakula will come to Mongolia to revitalise Buddhism which had turned into an ardent belief as the people were suffering disenfranchisement of their religion since 1930s when the Communist regime began to decimate and destroy the monasteries. I realised that belief and resolve of an average Mongolian was firm and that with the arrival of Rinpoche Bakula they considered the redemption complete.

Mongolia was going through a tremendous pain and suffering with the changing times and decimation of Soviet Union as far as daily requirements were concerned. However the balm that the mere presence of Rinpoche Bakula and his efforts to revive the monasteries and the religious pride of the Mongols provided can neither be measured not easily recounted or understood. Every life he touched became a story.

I remember once late in the evening the then Vice President and my dear friend Gonchigdorj called me to say that he had lost his father and his mother was highly disconsolate and he wanted to bring his mother for blessings by the Rinpoche. I knew well that by that time Rinpoche would have retired to his chambers which was also his bedroom, temple and meditation room and no one could disturb his Tapasya. I was in a fix as I also needed my Ambassador to avail such a wonderful opportunity to oblige the Vice President. I called his personal staff Lama Dawaji who was only authorised to go in. Even he was also unwilling to disturb the Ambassador in the state of meditation. I could not enter the chambers. Sonam was away to Beijing but I had already promised Gonchigdorj and hence virtually pushed Dawa ji to inform the Ambassador which he very unwillingly did. As a diplomat you don't get such opportunities very often. We were waiting for Rinpoche in his drawing room as both Ambassador and I lived on the first floor of the Embassy itself. After about 15 minutes Rinpoche came down and without a word blessed the Vice President and his mother in the traditional Buddhist manner. While leaving he also gave me a look that I could not forget. But I believed that interrupting his mediation has actually served the national cause rather effectively as the Vice President Gonchigdorj often spoke to me about this. The bereaved family appeared to be at peace.

Let me also tell you about the first day of my arrival in Ulaanbaatar by a long train journey from Hong Kong and Beijing. After I paid my respect to the ambassador, my predecessor invited me for a lunch at his house and around 3:30 PM. He casually mentioned that there is a press conference of the trade minister at 4:00 PM. I asked him why we were not going. And, he said that nothing much might come out of it. But I insisted and we went there. Since we were a little late we met the Mongolian Trade Minister in the lobby. He was Mr P Ochirbat who eventually rose to become the President of the country. He had welcomed me and remained kind throughout his tenure and helped us enhance bilateral ties even more.

As for Rinpoche Bakula, it was indeed for his immense contributions to the motherland he was conferred with Padma Bhushan award- not that any awards mattered to him. On their part the Mongolian leadership and Mongolian people who loved Indians felt blessed with the most unique Indian Ambassador and a saint in Rinpoche Bakula who stayed there for almost a decade. In recognition of his exemplary and yeoman services to the Mongolian nation and people the Mongolian Government conferred upon him their highest "Polar Star" award. In fact President P Ochirbat, who was the first President of democratic Mongolia paid great tributes to Rinpoche and I quote "Ambassador Bakula Rinpoche was a stateman, a diplomat and Buddhist clergy who carved out his own niche in the history of Mongolia. He recognised the historic necessity to develop Mongolia's national culture to restore the glory of Buddhism- an inseparable part of its cultural heritage. He was a divine messenger at the time of peaceful transformation from communism to democracy and a source of inspiration to our people."

We only used to have two capacity building slots under the ITEC program for training in India. But within a very short time the Ministry of External Affairs made it open ended. It has gone a long way in nurturing the appreciation of modern India with modern Mongolia.

We also did not have any companies from India working in Mongolia. But after a few months of my arrival we had the first business delegation led by CEO CIMMCO International, a Birla group company and then we had many others. India for the first time also extended the line of credit to Mongolia beyond its immediate neighbourhood. Now we have even extended more than $ 1bn in Lines of credit for a refinery project. Today we have several major companies working in Mongolia in diverse areas.

We are indeed neighbours and that too spiritual neighbours which is far more potent than simply being within the geographies. James Baker III, US Secretary of State, often used to tell the liberated Mongolians that US was its 3rd neighbour after Russia and China. But then we are in a different orbit altogether.

At that time India also helped Mongolia draft its constitution and we had the privilege of having justice Bhagwati, former Chief Justice of the Indian Supreme Court, helping the Mongolian government and discussing with them the future course of their constitutional journey. Large number of delegations preceded in different areas to render whatever assistance was possible when the country was going through its very difficult transition.

I have not spoken about the trade and investment and other geo political and geo economic matters for the simple reason that we have an exceptionally brilliant and authoritative line up of the speakers who know the conditions much more than I would and the areas in which India can collaborate and the Indian companies can find useful partnerships as both our countries move towards an AI driven industrial revolution 4.0. In my view the possibilities are immense from trade to tourism to investment to technology to capacity building where we are yet to achieve the potential. Mongolia is one of the most exciting investment opportunities currently available in the world. With over $10 billion USD already committed for deep mining and infrastructure projects, Mongolia remains the final frontier for investors to benefit from continual and rapid growth.

India herself is going through a tremendous change and economic upheaval and revival which has been necessitated by the fight against the pandemic. India has been the pharmacy of the world and a global vaccine hub. As you are aware India was probably the first country to provide medical assistance and the vaccines to the world when it needed these most. The fight is not over and India continues it locally and internationally in order to forge an international solidarity - an action plan without which the disadvantaged countries will not be able to recover from the ill effects of the pandemic. Pharmacy is also the bridge between India and Mongolia. India's gifting of 150,000 doses of Covid Vaccine on Feb 22, 2021 was billed as a "historic" moment by Mongolian Deputy Prime Minister, as it was Mongolia's first vaccine that came from India. The unique trust and potential between the two can lead us to much greater heights and depths of friendship, cooperation and collaboration in bilateral, regional and global context as it encompasses economic, political, defence and other strategic dimensions.

Once again, I would like to my express gratitude to the organisers and wish this conference a great success and actionable outcomes. I do look forward to be educated more from the distinguished presentations.

*****

Preface

Historical and economic conditions in both Mongolia and India have played a crucial role in fostering their vibrant relationship evidenced today. Geopolitical developments in their neighborhood and the forces of globalization will play ever larger roles than they did previously in shaping this relations. Such factors may differ in varying degrees from one state to another, but there also may be relevant similarities in the situations of both of them.

In view of the dramatic changes that have taken place in international politics and in both South and North-East Asia since the 1990's, interaction between and among the states of this wide region have developed opportunities to fashion ties with countries within and beyond the former Communist bloc. Also, diverse circumstances and trends in the world outside the boundaries of the former Communist bloc, particularly the expansion of the European Union, the future of NATO and emergence of China as a global player have all impacted on the bilateral relations of Mongolia and India.

Keeping in mind the developments in the Indo-Pacific and India's Look East and Look North Policies, New Vision University, Georgia, and Praghna Centre for Research, Coimbatore, India, came together to host a webinar with three specific goals:

The webinar sought to identify the factors that have affected and will affect the relations of Mongolia and India, as well as any or all of the states that are located in Greater Central Asia and the Turkic world to foster discussion of these factors by exchanging ideas and differing viewpoints.

The webinar included within the scope of its scholarly concerns the policies of national governments, international organizations and non-governmental groups which have a bearing on Asian international relations. The intent was to combine the interests of scholars from a variety of methodological perspectives and traditions, drawing on broad range of schools of thought as diverse as great power realism, national security studies, intelligence studies, and a number of different approaches.

The Editors believe that there are increasing opportunities to engage in meaningful discussions with a growing number of scholars from Eurasia which includes the Turkic world, Russosphere and Indosphere. Through their efforts, the Editors hope to facilitate the development of vigorous networks of communication and collaborative research among scholars working in the foreign policies of the post-Communist states.

We believe that this volume containing eight papers presented in the webinar by scholars and their thought processes will stimulate further research and exchange of scholarly communications to enhance our understanding of India's relations with Mongolia, other parts of Central Asia in the new geopolitical order that is emerging in the region now.

Professor Sureyya Yigit
Dr R Srinivasan

Editor's Note

This volume is a collation of the papers presented during the webinar on India-Mongolia Relations: Beyond Greater Central Asia held in July 2021.

Together, these eight papers present debates that engage the minds of emerging scholarship in India and abroad relating to concerns on economic, strategic and international order dimensions in India's relations with Mongolia and Greater Central Asia. Editors hope that publishing these thought processes, in the manner in which they were presented, as a compilation of Conference Proceedings in this volume will promote further research and greater interaction amongst the scholarly community.

Acknowledgement

Praghna Centre for Research wishes to place on record our gratitude to Prof. Sureyya Yigit of New Vision University, for his enthusiasm and exceptional cooperation in the conduct of the webinar and in the production of this volume. We are delighted to have him as Editor for this Volume. We acknowledge and thank Ambassador Anil Trigunayat and Air Marshal Matheswaran for sharing with us their important insights on a dimension that has profound strategic implications for both India and Mongolia. We also wish to convey our appreciation and gratitude to Professor RP Pradhan, BITS-Pilani Goa Campus for chairing a Session and presenting his incisive insights and his encouragement for bringing out this volume.

We also acknowledge the authors for their participation in the conference and contributing their written works making a wholesome contribution to this volume.

Professor Sureyya Yigit　　　　Dr R Srinivasan

Introduction

The buzzword of the past few decades has undoubtedly been globalisation which cannot be reduced to expanding networks dominated by Western political, economic, ideological, technological and financial systems. If their dominance is indisputable, as was the supremacy of the American hyperpower, the global chessboard is not a zero-sum game. The international discussions concerning multipolarity attenuated as American unilateralism began to assert itself under the Bush presidency. However, it was wrong to believe in the ongoing subjugation of the powers in the second circle: European Union, Russia, China, and Japan.

In this context, the Indian case is worthy of interest for several reasons. It first testifies to the new ambition of a state of one billion inhabitants, a beacon country of decolonisation, and then a leader of the non-aligned movement. The economic reform initiated in 1991 and the nuclear tests of 1998 testify to the distinct but complementary modes of a desire to be part of a global game that New Delhi wishes to see extended to new players.

The Indian case also sheds light on the ambiguity of self-affirmation dynamics. The protest path, denouncing the injustices of the world order, calls for a redefinition of a more balanced world architecture. It thus anchors itself in the contesting tradition of the critical post-colonial heritage. Very quickly, however, this same discussion is coupled with the affirmation of a nation, which is much less the founding paradigm of India in the 1950s and 1960s, which can be defined as "Nehruvian idealism", than a return to Lord Palmerston's famous dictum: "Countries do not have permanent friends. They only have permanent interests."

Governments in power in New Delhi fully assumed this logic of realpolitik in the service of national interests. However, they did so in a contemporary space-time dialectic based on three arguments:

- The concept of a "resurgent" India anchors today's ambitions in a remote past: it is carried by an identity-based reading of history promoting the concept of Hinduism and invoking, at least implicitly, the golden age of pre-Islamic Hindu kingdoms.
- This vision of the world bears, as it should, a particular interest in the macro-regional context, which is to say, in Asian geopolitics and its major poles concerning the Indian interests: the Pakistani-Afghan continuum, China, Russia, Central Asia, and the coastal and maritime strip that runs from the Middle East to Indonesia.

- India is projecting itself into the globalised world by displaying itself there in new and promising forms through a diaspora that asserts itself in scientific, technological, cultural and economic fields.

Consequently, the world seen from New Delhi is not only governed by an unequal order. It also offers opportunities to advance Indian interests and reshape India's image in its region and beyond. Questioning how India sees the world requires also questioning how it sees itself. In both cases, the singular is reductive. There are pluralities of perceptions, as there should be, a fortiori in a state of more than a billion inhabitants, a parliamentary democracy with a veritable intellectual tradition equipped with a pluralist press, a large political class structured in multiple parties, and a galaxy of non-governmental organisations, many of which have achieved international renown. In this sense, "the world seen from New Delhi" is a reductive formula favouring government decision-makers analysis.

However, behind this polyphony, some dominant lines emerge. These are the ones one needs to identify here, emphasising from the outset a major theme: the transition, even of a paradigm change. Briefly, the 1990s marked the transition from post-colonial India, which gained independence in 1947, to what may be termed a post-post-colonial India: giving up one relatively defensive position (marked by economic protectionism) to a lateral one (non-alignment) to assert its interests and ambitions in a new tone, in a world where India's influential position is considered inadequate when one compares its modesty with the historical weight of Indian civilisation, and with the demographic weight of India today.

The nuclear tests conducted in the late 1990s are the most striking signal of this new vision of oneself and the world. However, they only endorsed, adding a specific ideological colour, a deeper, less partisan process. The beginning of the economic reform, launched in 1991 by the Congress Party, the standard bearer of the anti-colonial movement, a then major builder of the new nation, remains, in fact, the most significant symbol of this entry into a new phase, which is based on a reading of oneself and of the order of the world which does not deny the past, but which bears witness to a profound transformation. Without waiting for poverty to be reabsorbed, India intends to leave behind its image as a developing country and a fortiori as an underdeveloped country, assert itself as an emerging market, and display its ambitions for power.

Nehru's Idealism and Contemporary Realpolitik

When India gained independence in 1947, Jawaharlal Nehru, Prime Minister until he died in 1964, intended both to forge the new nation and to actively define his country's place in the world while preserving before him the portfolio of Foreign Affairs. He was one of the primary promoters of non-alignment, challenging the bloc logic since the Korean War while asserting at the same time values which combined universalism and the concern to preserve national sovereignty. Nourished by multiple influences, his political philosophy also bears the indelible mark of colonial exploitation. This experience partly explains the economic choices that he made, which implemented a regime of a mixed economy. Planning, nationalisations and a large public sector do not, however, make India a socialist state: the market economy, even if regulated, reigned over the majority of transactions. As for protectionism, it took the opposite course to the history of India, opening up to the large Western trading companies from the 17th century, culminating with the political domination of the East India Company, which made the subcontinent the flagship of the British Empire.

Nehru's India appeared at the Bandung Conference in 1955 as the theoretician of non-alignment. She liked to present herself as the spokesperson for new nations or soon-to-be independent and occasionally suggested that its size, historical experience and rhetorical ability enabled it to say what smaller countries still dared not say. A discreet scent of self-proclaimed messianism floated over Indian diplomacy, rejecting classic colonialism and modern imperialism's neo-colonial forms. As early as 1950, the United States rejected this position in the name of an all too familiar binary principle: "either you are with us or against us". Such a misunderstanding did not prevent Washington from establishing a policy of economic aid to prevent India, after China, from experiencing a socialist revolution.

The war with China in 1962 sounded the death knell for Nehruvian foreign policy, reminding the country humiliated by rapid defeat that power relations also governed international relations. Indira Gandhi certainly remembered this. Two years after consolidating power over factions of the Congress Party opposed to its pre-eminence, she intervened militarily in East Pakistan in 1971 to help the secession, which gave birth to Bangladesh. Displaying a theoretical non-alignment which gave way in practice, as in 1971, to a treaty of friendship with the USSR, which it was careful not to criticise after the entry of Soviet troops into Afghanistan in 1979.

Post-Cold War

The major turning point dates from 1991, when two different events collided: the collapse of the USSR and the Indian financial crisis. This led the Congress party, freshly victorious in the elections after the assassination of Rajiv Gandhi, to further question the country's economic policy, which had been debated since the 1980s. The old economic model was in crisis and much criticised for blocking, under the empire of regulation, various initiatives, productivity and competitiveness. As for the collapse of the USSR, it marked the end of the bloc policy and the weakening of an essential supplier in terms of armaments and of a significant partner in terms of trade, accepting in part the barter and the non-convertible rupee.

This translated to taking a new glance at itself and a new look at the world: India had to reform for herself and not disconnect from a world where liberalism was ascendant. However, the thesis of the so-called end of history appealed neither to Indian policymakers nor to the intelligentsia. However, it extolled the unsurpassable merits of democracy because it gave too much credence to economic liberalism that did not fit well with the Indian heritage of a mixed economy. Liberalising the Indian economy, to all governments of the 1990s who saw virtually the entire political spectrum gaining responsibilities, meant working to break down bureaucratic locks to promote better productivity; it did not mean renouncing the regulation of the economy. Although India had to embark in 1991 on a structural adjustment program demanded by the IMF in order to obtain the loans requested, the path followed in no way resembled the Russian experience for many reasons: India knew what the market was, her economy restarted in 1992, and her negotiating ability was strong when facing the supporters of the "Washington Consensus" who governed the World Bank and the International Monetary Fund.

The logic of nuclearisation is also part of a dialectic on several dimensions. It proceeds from a reading of the regional environment, marked by a delicate relationship with China, a relationship which refers to a much broader horizon, enveloping the whole of Asia, its Russian and Middle Eastern neighbours, and the U.S. policy in the region. In the doubly asymmetrical triangle that governs relations between India, Pakistan and China, nuclearisation, which promotes deterrence from the weak to the strong, is thought to benefit Pakistan rather than India, which is superior to it on the conventional arms level. On the other hand, India's signal sent to China takes on its full meaning for precisely the same reasons. Suppose China is in every way- militarily, economically, diplomatically - more powerful than India. In that case, the latter raises its status by becoming a nuclear power, even if it means arousing protests from Beijing. When the Indian Prime Minister, in a letter to President Clinton, argued in May 1998 of the strategy of a "northern neighbour" which would encircle his country, helping Pakistan's nuclear program and pushing its pawns into Myanmar. The cold front did not last long, and Sino-Indian relations resumed their usual course, marked by several ulterior motives.

Despite the soothing speeches of Beijing, India continued to be concerned regarding the increases in the Chinese arsenal. As for China, the condescension with which it usually judges India is diminishing, especially since an India on better terms with the United States, and more active in Southeast Asia, can serve as a counterweight to her own ambitions. India guards its positive relationship with Russia after a softening phase carried out under the Presidency of Boris Yeltsin.

Indo-Russian military cooperation regained colour and effectiveness. However, India did not pretend to compete with its big neighbours; it knew it did not yet play in the same category.

In short, while waiting for better days, India wishes to see its role as a regional power challenged by a weakened, albeit nuclear, Pakistan and intends to be able to exert a new influence in what it defines as being its "strategic space", "Looking North", where its vital interests are deployed: This includes South Asia, of course, but also the maritime horizon which runs from the Gulf to the Strait of Malacca, and Central Asia, both as a possible source of energy supply and to counter possible Pakistani ambitions. The sirens of a Russian-Sino-Indian strategic triangle thwarting the Western thrust may have stunned some Indian watchers for a time when Primakov launched such a hypothesis. Indian diplomacy, for its part, is aware of Chinese reluctance in this regard. Furthermore, above all, the time for anti-Americanism is over. Russia of Vladimir Putin testifies in multiple mannerisms in challenging the United States and NATO by advancing an aggressive war against Ukraine, hoping for relative withdrawal by the West, which it believes will preserve its vital interests for the future.

While keeping in mind the multifaceted bubbling emanating from civil society, and its divergent positions, one can conclude by returning to what is defined as the dominant spirit of India today, which bears both the political forces in power and, beyond partisan affiliations, the largely consensual space occupied by those who wish to see India assert itself in the world of tomorrow. From the power in place today, one must retain an altogether pragmatic line which does not concern transcendent principles.

India ultimately illustrates its capacity for dialectics, inscribed in its intellectual tradition. In a world that still needs to recognise the place it would like to occupy and whose economic power it knows is the necessary, if not sufficient, level, India plays on several scales and in several stages. The turns seem quick: especially the rapprochement with the United States. In truth, these turns are dictated by a sense of opportunity, which bears in mind the end goal. In the transition phase in which it was engaged, India got closer to Washington while criticising its disguised protectionism and its Pakistani policy. Nevertheless, this commitment was not alignment, although New Delhi chose to remain silent on certain points which would have shocked it in the past: for example, the concept of the axis of evil or that of preventive war. It is a matter of American hegemony as it is of the World Trade Organization: it was considered better to be part of it or take advantage of it - even if it meant seeking the best possible balance between the adaptations to be made, the country's capacity to adopt the reforms, and the attempts to overhaul the international system itself. India has always aimed towards the objective of multipolarity; hence the United States approach has tended to be seen by other countries as some in India as an attempt to impose American values and credentials - whether on human rights, nuclear proliferation or of missiles, of multilateral commercial stakes, of the rights of intellectual property to name some. In the East, several countries, notably India, as well as Russia and China, have expressed their reservations about some of these developments, with such asymmetries requiring a coalition of interests between equals rather than alliances built around hegemony,

In the long term, India implies that it thinks of finding its rightful place in the world system. This conviction requires an effort on oneself, of which no one knows when it will be brought to fruition nor how it will affect the nation's spirit. One thing is certain, however: the India of the 1990s criticised the powers and their unequal order. However, it is indeed their ranks that it intends to integrate in the second decade of the twenty-first century.

India: Regional Actor

India redefined its regional policy at the end of the cold war for three main reasons. There was a need to end her international isolation, linked to the loss of her primary partner for economics and defence: The Soviet Union. The second was the fear of an increase in the Chinese presence in South and Southeast Asia. Third, Prime Minister Narasimha Rao initiated the liberalisation of India's economy. These changes led, during the 1990s, to the recalibration of regional policy in India around the concept of a "distant neighbourhood", which returned to the idea that India had to break up the borders of South Asia.

The distant neighbourhood of India's east was thought of in concentric circles, from its immediate vicinity, the South Asian peninsula, to Southeast Asia, the Middle East and the southern Indian Ocean. This reconceptualisation of foreign policy and defence of India was initially based on strengthening economic ties with his distant neighbours, which culminated by the beginning of the 2000s through the establishment of bilateral strategic partnerships with countries from South East Asia and with the Middle East (Gulf Cooperation Council countries, Israel and Iran).

This notion of "distant neighbourhood" is gradually being replaced by the "Indo-Pacific space", which appeared in the late 2000s focusing on the influence of the rapprochement of India with the United States and Japan. Here the main idea was the protection of common goods, trade, of the freedom of use of the seas. The goal was of a Maritime India in opposition to Beijing's policy of territorial expansion in the South China Sea.

Integrating this notion into Indian political discussions testifies to one redefinition by New Delhi of its area of strategic priority in a strategic continuum that extends from the Indian Ocean to the Pacific Ocean and extends to Japan and Australia. The notion of the Indo-Pacific space is a concept that is both geopolitical and geoeconomic, shared by the U.S., Japan, Australia, India and, more recently, France, which is emerging largely as a result of the growing Chinese presence in the Indian Ocean. Instead of creating a division between the Indian and Pacific Oceans or between South Asia and Southeast Asia, the notion of the Indo-Pacific encourages us to think of this super-region as a unit, an interconnected geostrategic space. This idea may not just be a new label applied to the Asia-Pacific but an acknowledgment of economic and strategic changes which recognise the acceleration of economic connections between the peaceful West and the Indian Ocean, which contributes to creating a singular strategic system.

For India in particular, the Indian Ocean is central to guarantee her security in terms of commerce and energy: more than 90 % of India's foreign trade by volume, and 70 % in value, pass in effect by this maritime route. The roots of these changes may be economical, but they are also linked to strategic factors, among which the increase in Sino-Indian competition has been decisive. The conceptualisation of this transregional maritime space also contains a strong normative dimension; who aims to oppose the Chinese Belt and Road Initiative with Western values? The Japanese and American powers were the first to employ the notion of a free and open Indo-Pacific space during the latter half of the 2010s.

In line with such contemporary developments, this book focuses on eight specific dimensions of an important bilateral relationship: India and Mongolia. They are the latest developments in the bilateral relationship, Mongolia's relations with Russia, India as Mongolia's third neighbour, Mongolia's relations with the United States, contemporary bilateral relations, Tajik Indian relations, soft power between India and Mongolia and lastly, India and Tajikistan as ancient Civilisations.

Stephen P. Westcott writing about "Closing the Blindspot between India's Look East and Look North Policies: Recent Developments in Indo-Mongolian Relations", highlights the nearly three-quarter-century relationship as being negligible throughout the decades. Lack of mutual interest and differing foreign policy aims have contributed to this. Neither country appeared in the foreign policy milieu of the other as an aspiring collaborative partner. The past decade has witnessed a surge in the relationship with India's aspirations and Mongolia's natural resources playing a key role.

In my chapter entitled "Mongolia's Historic Relations with its Largest Neighbour: Russia," I explore the rich and wide-ranging relationship the two countries have enjoyed throughout the centuries. The chapter is effectively divided into two parts, with the first highlighting the origins of the relationship with a keen focus on Tsarist times. The second part investigates the period after the collapse of the Soviet Union. This is categorised under three stages. The initial stage signifies severe decline, the second stage is where stabilisation occurs, and the third stage emanates in recovery. Given that the two countries are neighbours sharing a border of 3,485 km which makes up 42.7% of Mongolia's total border, cross-border trade and cooperation becomes highly significant, especially with Buryatia, an ethnic Mongol group native to south-eastern Siberia who speak the Buryat language and form a republic in the Russian Federation. This is studied in detail in the last part of the chapter.

Dr RP Pradhan in his chapter "Small is Not Vulnerable: India in Mongolia's Third Neighbour Dilemma" reminds us that nearly a thousand years ago, Mongolians ruled parts of present-day Russia and China. However, by the mid-14th century, this giant empire began to disintegrate. At the peak of Pax Mongolica, Mongolia had an almost unending empire. If one were to compare the size of Pax Mongolica in modern terms, its territory would expand over thirty countries today, consisting of a population of approximately 3 billion. Contemporary Mongolia is the precise opposite of its historical past in many dimensions. This chapter explores small states' security vulnerabilities by offering normative explanations and investigates whether Mongolia can draw lessons from Switzerland, Djibouti and Singapore to negotiate its vulnerability.

Sanchana Srivastava investigates "The United States and Mongolia Relations: The Underrated Partnership" and underscores the fact that the U.S. has consistently supported Mongolian democracy, which can be seen as a positive example to other regional states. The post-cold war bilateral relationship is not solely limited to the ideals of liberal democracy but is based on practical benefits to both countries. The relationship is not based purely on ideology but on realpolitik, whereby deeper entrenched relations should be centred on the practical benefits each party will gain from the partnership.

Dr Mukesh H. Khatik and Ms Upasana Bhandari probe "Indo-Mongolian Relations in Present Era", suggesting that the two countries benefit from a good synergy, especially the historical and cultural impact of Buddhism on how it continues to build mutual relations. Mongolia considers India, a spiritual neighbour who desires to see its partner flourish and prosper in strengthening democratic traditions and institutions. Within the bilateral relationship, special attention is directed at the political and security partnership on bilateral defence, security, commercial, economic, border patrolling, disaster management, energy, cultural and technical cooperation, foreign policy support and consultations, humanitarian assistance, medical missions, and a digital connectivity network.

Dr Pravesh Kumar Gupta writes about "Situating Tajikistan in India's Central

Asia Policy: A Strategic Dimension", assessing the significance of Tajikistan as an aspect of India's extended neighbourhood policy, alongside the critical examination of regional factors affecting their relations. This perspective focuses on political, trade and economic Relations, emphasising investments and connectivity, developmental partnership and capacity-building. Concerning the security dimension within the India-Tajikistan Relationship, the convergence of interests in countering terrorism and extremism is investigated. Both countries have emphasised the enhanced dialogue between their security agencies and regular meetings at the Foreign Ministers level to discuss pressing regional security issues.

Anagha Babu focuses on "A Fiddle, A Horse and A Bodhi Tree Sapling: The Role of Soft Power Diplomacy in Indo-Mongolian Relations", underlining that Indian soft power has been of enormous advantage for its foreign policy. India has a chance of becoming a world power sometime in the future due to its vast and varied soft power elements despite its social inequalities and poverty. It has successfully portrayed itself as a nation of rich culture, history, heritage and unique philosophy. Nevertheless, India has not yet fully realised its soft power potential. This chapter examines the sources of India's soft power and the role of soft power in bilateral relations and suggests policy recommendations in this area, potentially augmenting Indian soft power.

Narendra Sharma provides the final chapter entitled "India-Tajikistan Relations: From Civilizational Friends to Strategic Partners", concentrating on shared history, culture and civilisational links. In modern times, such ties have been driven by the convergence of geopolitical concerns and interests. Threat perceptions were radically altered by the Taliban takeover of Afghanistan, with regular diplomatic consultations resulting in closer defence cooperation. Geography, the lack of a direct land connection, has proved to be a major hurdle, especially in the economic and trade dimension. Attention is given to the entry of India to the Shanghai Cooperation Organisation, whereby the challenges of radicalisation, state-sponsored terrorism, the withdrawal of foreign troops from Afghanistan and the possible return of Taliban have accelerated the impetus to cooperate in the fields of security, defence, trade and diplomacy.

Professor Sureyya Yigit
New Vision University,
Tbilisi, Georgia

1. Closing the Blindspot between India's Look East and Look North Policies: Recent Developments in Indo-Mongolian Relations

Stephen P. Westcott[1]

Abstract

Despite nearly 75 years of bilateral relations, India and Mongolia's engagements have been remained negligible throughout much of this time. This has been in part due to a lack of convergence in their shared interests and in part to disparate foreign policy priorities. Even after the Cold War ended and both states sought to expand their international relations, neither state considered the other a serious avenue for further partnership. India's Look East Policy and Look North Policy, in which it refocused its foreign policy towards South East/East Asia and Central Asia respectively, left Mongolia on the periphery of both regions. Mongolia for its part has adopted a 'third neighbour' policy that mostly focused on the USA and Northeast Asian states. However, since 2010, Indo-Mongolian relations have seen a notable surge in engagement, with increased frequency and depth of diplomatic, economic development and military engagements. This paper explores the recent growth in Indo-Mongolian relations in order to identify and explain the factors behind it. Specifically, I posit here that a blend of India's rise as a regional great power, the growth in Mongolia's resource sector, and China's increasing assertiveness has pushed both states into each other's circles and will likely sustain their engagement into the immediate future.

Keywords: India, Mongolia, Look/Act East Policy; Look North Policy; Third Neighbour Policy

1 Stephen P. Westcott is a Postdoctoral Fellow in the College of Arts, Business, Law and Social Sciences, Murdoch University. Email: stephen.westcott@murdoch.edu.au

Introduction:

In May 2015, Narendra Modi became the first Indian Prime Minister to visit Mongolia, signifying a significant breakthrough in the two state's bilateral relations. During Modi's state visit, thirteen different treaties and Memorandum of Understandings were signed, India extended to Mongolia a US$1 billion Line of Credit to construct an oil refinery and Indian-Mongolian relations were officially elevated to the 'strategic partnership' level (MEA, 2015). This flurry of activity has been built upon in the subsequent six years since Modi's visit, generating an unprecedented depth and breadth of Indo-Mongolian diplomatic and development engagement. Although India's economic and political engagement with Mongolia are dwarfed by Mongolia's neighbours, as well as Japan and the USA, both states are clearly placing increasing emphasis and effort into expanding their bilateral relationship (Krishna, 2020; Soni, 2016).

Geopolitically speaking, this is an interesting development. The two states are separated by approximately 3600 kilometres of mountainous terrain and open wilderness. Furthermore, Mongolia is landlocked country far from the sea, completely surrounded by Russia to the north and China to the south. Naturally, this has limited India and Mongolia's ability to trade or establish strong channels of communication. Indeed, for most of their history as independent nations, there have been only fleeting and tokenistic engagements between the two states. Even after the Cold War ended and both states began actively expanding their foreign engagements, Mongolia existed in something of a blind spot for Indian foreign policy. Post-Communist Mongolia for its part indicated an interest in developing stronger ties with India as part of its foreign policy although it prioritised seeking friendly relations with 'highly developed' countries, a category it clearly did not consider India to be part of. This immediately begs the question: why have Indo-Mongolian relations seen such growth over the past decade?

Most scholarship on Indo-Mongolian relations identify the shared values of democracy and the cultural connection of Buddhism as the basis for the two countries post-Cold War relations (Batbayar, 2001; Kaplonski, 2004; Soni, 2015). Whilst these factors have clearly provided an important foundation and have been actively cultivated by India as a source of soft power to foster a strong sense of bonhomie between the two states, I argue that they are insufficient to account for the recent uptick in diplomatic engagement. Instead, I posit here that three geopolitical developments have driven this expansion of Indo-Mongolian relations. First is India's emergence as a regional great power in the past two decades, which has seen it actively engage and seek more of a leadership role in Central and East Asia. Second is Mongolia's mining boom which has seen it develop a sizeable mining industry and begin exporting minerals. Finally, China's increasing assertiveness in the region and towards India and Mongolia specifically has seen the two states begin to engage in hedging activities, exploring potential areas of security and political alignment without overtly seeking to balance their overmighty neighbour.

This article will unpack this argument in four main sections. The first two sections explore the Indian and Mongolian foreign policy and illustrates how their differing priorities in the initial post-Cold War period ensured that they rarely had much overlap. In particular it is illustrated here how Mongolia fell into a blind spot for Indian policymakers whilst Mongolia simply had other priorities that required its limited resources. The third section focus on how the Indo-Mongolian relationship developed in the post-Cold War period, with specific emphasis on how bilateral engagements have grown in breadth and depth since 2010. Here it is shown how the relationship has grown from primarily cultural exchanges to more robust intergovernmental cooperation and executive level engagement on many projects. Finally, the three geopolitical factors of India's rise, Mongolia's resource boom and China's assertiveness are discussed to illustrate why India and Mongolia have grown increasingly close as their interests align yet still find an actual alliance infeasible and unattractive.

India Overlooks Mongolia

Throughout much of their history as independent states, Mongolia has represented something of a blind spot for Indian engagement with Asia. During the Cold War era, this was largely due the fact that they walked in different spheres of influence and allegiance. Since 1922, Mongolia acted as a loyal vasal state of the Soviet Union and remained firmly in the Soviet bloc, even flirting with the idea of formally joining the USSR at several stages (Narangoa, 2009, p. 363). In contrast, since it gained its independence, India mostly pursued a non-aligned policy, seeking to maintain its strategic autonomy even as it increasingly favoured the Soviet Union (Ganguly & Pardesi, 2009). This ensured that even though India was the first state outside of the communist bloc to formally recognise Mongolia in December 1955, actual diplomatic engagements between the two states were kept to a minimum. Indeed, India neglected to establish a diplomatic mission in Ulaanbaatar until 1971 and, other than India sponsoring Mongolia's entry into the United Nations in 1961, bilateral or multilateral interactions between the two states were rare (MEA, 2021).

Although the potential for greater breadth and depth of India-Mongolia relations was opened following the collapse of the Soviet Union in 1991, the geopolitical shockwave ensured that India was focused on other priorities. Specifically, India's largest source of trade and military supplies disappeared almost overnight, leaving it on the verge of default. In response, India radically reformed and restructured its economic and foreign policies, most notably developing the 'Look East' policy. Essentially, the Look East policy involved India coordinated pivot from its previous focus on great power politics and the Non-Aligned Movement to actively engage with its previously neglected Asian neighbourhood. Initially, the impetus of the policy was to develop trade partnerships make up for the loss of the USSR and attract investment in India to assist with the modernisation of its increasingly obsolete infrastructure. Whilst in theory this policy could has seen India engage with the all of the Asian-Pacific region, the clear focus for India was the ASEAN states as well as the 'Asian Tiger' economies which in the 1990s were at their height (Acharya, 2015, pp. 455–457; Sikri, 2009, pp. 132–133).

The 'Look East' quickly became the flagship foreign policy for Indian diplomacy in the 1990s and 2000s as successive governments embraced it. As it matured, the Look East policy increasingly developed political and strategic as well as economic objectives as India sought to utilise the policy as its main framework for engaging with Asia and deepen the connections that it made (Ganguly & Pardesi, 2009, pp. 13–14; Sikri, 2009). It also expanded to cover non-ASEAN states, notably deepening relations with China, Japan, South Korea and later Australia. Shortly after their election in 2014, the Modi government rebranded the policy as 'Act East' indicating that it wanted to inject more dynamism into the policy. However, it is worth noting here that this proven to be little more than a PR stunt as there was no significant change in level or focus India's engagement with Southeast and East Asia (Bajpaee, 2017; Ganapathi, 2015).

A lesser-known regional policy of India's was the 'Look North' policy, the *de facto* approach through which India attempted to engage with the Central Asian states. Fundamentally the Look North policy sought to capitalise on the disintegration of the USSR by making coordinated diplomatic inroads into Central Asia, specifically with the former Soviet republics. India's primary aims here were to cultivate the Central Asian republics as partners against religious extremism and to gain access to the rich resources and potential markets in the region (Kavalski, 2010, pp. 80–84; Krishna, 2020, pp. 109–110). However, in contrast with the Look East policy, the landlocked nature of the Central Asian states and the established influence of Russia and China in the region ensured that the Look North policy was produced few tangible results. In response, in 2012 India revamped its regional engagement by launching the 'Connect Central Asia Policy' in an attempt to reinvigorate efforts to partner with Central Asian states to develop stronger trade and commercial ties. This revamped policy has seen closer military and economic cooperation between India and many of the Central Asian states, especially after Prime Minister Modi's 2015 tour of the region. Nonetheless, problems with establishing a direct route for trade have ensured that India has been unable to provide a genuine alternative partner for Central Asian states (Kavalski, 2015, pp. 429–430; Wani, 2020, pp. 20–25).[2]

Notwithstanding the success or failures of either the Look East or Look North policies, Mongolia was not an easy fit for India's main regional policies geopolitically speaking. Indeed, there was no clear consensus within the Indian government and pundits as to whether Mongolia should be considered to as part of Northeast Asia, Central Asia or both (Kavalski, 2015, p. 425; Krishna, 2020, p. 101), indicating that it has been on the periphery of both in India's perspective. Although the Modi government eventually included it under the umbrella of the Act East policy in 2015, Mongolia was more frequently simply overlooked and not considered in Indian engagement with either region. Thus, with little to draw India's gaze during the 1990s and 2000s, Mongolia effectively fell into a blind spot in India's foreign policy, thereby ensuring that it remained largely neglected and Indo-Mongolian ties remained stunted during this period.

The Mongolian Foreign Policy

Generally speaking, Mongolia has been viewed by scholars and observers as more interested in developing a close relationship with India (Batbayar, 2001; Soni, 2016). However, initially post-communist Mongolia showed little interest in actively courting India. With the disintegration of the USSR, Mongolia effectively lost its suzerain which had underpinned its security and economy since 1922. Mongolia itself also bowed to popular domestic pressure in 1990 and transitioned relatively smoothly from a communist state into a multiparty democracy (Campi, 2018, pp. 62–63; Kaplonski, 2004, pp. 50–70). However, the new regime was initially focused upon stabilising its domestic situation and establishing its political institutions, ensuring that engagement with the international community outside of its neighbours and major organisations was limited. Indeed, it was only in 1994 that the Mongolian Great Hural (its unicameral parliament) turned its attention in earnest to establishing the principles guiding how the new republic's foreign policy should be conducted. The result of this deliberation was the passing of its first 'Concept of Mongolia's Foreign Policy' which, despite some minor revisions in 2011, has provided the stable foundation and framework through which Mongolia has conducted its external affairs (Reeves, 2012, pp. 590–591; Soni, 2020, pp. 65–68).[3]

2 To avoid confusion, these the Look East and Look North policies will be referred to their original rather than their current names throughout this paper.

3 Mongolia simultaneously adopted the 'Concept of National Security' and in the following year the 'Fundamentals of Military Doctrine' which essentially just outlined what it would consider to be a threat to its national interests and how it sought to use its security forces to defend them. These documents complement the Concept of

Whilst addressing a wide array of considerations, the salient points of Mongolia's Foreign Policy Concept is that it committed to maintaining a "open and non-aligned" stance in international relations whilst avoiding "becoming overly reliant or dependent on any particular country" (MJIA, 1995, p. 57). In outlining the political considerations, the Concept specified that Mongolia's independent foreign policy would focus first and foremost on developing good relations with China and Russia, maintaining "good neighbourly cooperation" and "a balanced relationship with both of them" (MJIA, 1995, p. 58). The second priority for Mongolia was to "develop friendly relations with highly developed countries of the West and East", before seeking to strengthen its political-economic position in Asia and engage with international organisations.

Thus, Mongolia developed a pragmatic multitiered foreign policy with the explicit aim of ensuring it avoids becoming dominated or beholden to any one state (Campi, 2018; Soni, 2015). Although there has been some debate about whether to declare Mongolia a 'permanently neutral' country like Switzerland (Campi, 2018, p. 88; Soni, 2020, pp. 71–73), the primary manifestation of this goal has been Mongolia's 'third neighbour' policy. In essence, the third neighbour policy has involved concerted efforts to cultivate close "bilateral and multilateral cooperation with highly developed democracies" (MFA, n.d., sec. 3.1.1.5). The clear aim of this policy has been not just to solicit economic and political investment into Mongolia, but also to balance or dilute the influence of its immediate neighbours Russia and China. Whilst India was explicitly mentioned in the Foreign Policy Concept as a state with which Mongolia should establish 'friendly relations' with, Ulaanbaatar clearly did not consider India a strong candidate to cultivate as a third neighbour. Indeed, for its first two decades as a democracy, Mongolia focused its diplomatic efforts on developing relations with the USA, the European Union, Japan and South Korea, not considering India to be within the same league (Narangoa, 2009, pp. 372–376; Soni, 2015, pp. 41–44).

The Recent Explosion Indo-Mongolian Relations

Whilst India's and Mongolia's interests and trajectories ensured that they rarely walked in the same circles, this is not to say that there was no notable engagement between the two states in the post-Cold War years. Indeed, there were several treaties signed between India and Mongolia during this period, including the 1994 Treaty of Friendly Relations and Cooperation and the 2001 signing of six sperate agreements covering defence and law enforcement cooperation (Krishna, 2020, p. 103; MEA, 2001). Arguably the most significant development in Indo-Mongolian

Foreign Policy in providing the foundational framework for Mongolia's independent international relations.

relations during this period, however, was India's assistance in restoring Buddhist institutions to Mongolia. Buddhism was actively repressed under Mongolia's communist regime but was recognised by the new republic as part of "the Mongolian people's intellectual civilisation" and made it a national security goal to "revive and develop Buddhist religion and culture" (MFA, n.d., sec. 3.1.4.7-8). Given India's historical-cultural inheritance as the birthplace of Buddhism and refuge of the Dali Lama, it was in a unique position to assist Mongolia with this goal. India's inspired choice to appoint a Buddhist monk, Kushok Bakula Rimpoche, to act as its ambassador between 1990 and 2000 also helped strengthen bilateral relations as he helped establish several monasteries and expand the Mongolian ecclesiastical cadre (Soni, 2016, pp. 55–56).

These agreements and cultural interactions provided a strong foundation for Indo-Mongolia relations, ensuring much good will between the two states and earning India the label 'spiritual neighbour.' Ultimately though, the engagements of this era generated little tangible economic or strategic developments and mostly consisted of tokenistic gestures such as renaming institutions or gifting copies sacred documents. Bilateral relations gradually grew closer and deeper throughout the 2000s as defence and law cooperation, especially following the initiation of Operation Nomadic Elephant, a joint military exercise between the two states that has been held roughly annually since 2004 (Defence News India, 2019). Yet, Indo-Mongolian relations remained sporadic and overshadowed by their relations with other states. Their bilateral relationship began to take on more impetus for both sides after they came to a civil nuclear agreement in September 2009 in which Mongolia agreed to allow the sale of uranium to India (Chandramohan, 2015; Soni, 2016, p. 57). Whilst little tangible came from this agreement,[4] it did act as the catalyst for the elevation of Indo-Mongolian relations to the 'comprehensive partnership' level and for Mongolia to identify India as a 'third neighbour' for the first time in 2010.

As a result of this elevated relationship, Indo-Mongolian relations saw a marked explosion in engagement throughout the 2010s under the mantra of the 'Three Ds': Dharma, Democracy and Development. One sign of this has been the increased frequency and calibre of state visits that each has paid to the other (Campi, 2018, pp. 86–87). Indeed, according a report by India's Ministry of External Affairs, there have been at least as many high level state visits in the past decade as there were in

4 This author has been unable to find any evidence of Mongolia actually exporting uranium or nuclear related material to India or that there has been any serious investment from India into its uranium mining sector. Indeed, according to the Observatory of Economic Complexity, Mongolia's trade with India is still dominated by the traditional agricultural sector, with wool, hides and other animal products being the predominant exports throughout the 2010s (OEC, 2021).

the previous 55 years of Indo-Mongolian relations (MEA, 2021). These state visits have also increasingly involved members of cabinet from both states' governments, rather than visits from the largely ceremonial positions of President or House Speaker which led previous visits from both countries. The most notable of these state visits was the previously mentioned state visit by Prime Minister Modi, the first ever visit by an Indian Prime Minister to Mongolia, although India's External Affairs Minister and Home Affairs Minister both separately visited Mongolia in 2018. Key members of Mongolia's government have also frequently visited India, including the Deputy Prime Minister (in 2016), the Foreign Minister (in 2016 and 2019), the Defence Minister (in 2018) and the Minister of Mining (in 2018).

Beyond the increase of high-profile visits, the Indo-Mongolian relationship has also gained greater depth and breadth as the number of dialogues and conferences between officials has ballooned. Arguably the most important of these intergovernmental dialogues is the India-Mongolia Joint Committee on Cooperation, a ministerial level meeting started in the 2000s but held roughly biannually since 2011.[5] The Joint Committee has been the primary mechanism used by India and Mongolia to coordinate the activities surrounding on their agreements and explore avenues where their partnership can be expanded upon (MEA, 2020, 2021). At time of writing, most recent meeting was the 7th Joint Committee Meeting which was held virtually in December 2020.

Intergovernmental department engagements have also been increasing. Of note, the Indian Border Security Force and the Mongolian General Authority on Border Protection have been frequently collaborating on issues of border management practices, conducting joint training exercises and other capacity building exercises since 2014 (MEA, 2021; PTI, 2018). India has also been active in assisting Mongolia develop other security capabilities including the assisting with the establishment of the Cyber Security Training Centre and conducting special forces training during Operation Nomadic Elephant and Mongolia's annual military exercise 'Khaan Quest' (Campi, 2018, pp. 78–79). There have been a proliferation of similar agreements between the relevant government bodies for joint projects in fields as diverse as space exploration, agriculture and medical research since 2015 (Bayasgalan & Jargalsaikhan, 2021; Krishna, 2020, pp. 106–107).

The economic and development engagements between India and Mongolia have also been increasingly blooming. Trade between India and Mongolia has grown from less than US$2.5 million in value in the mid-2000s to nearly US37 million in

5 This author has been unable to find any reference of the Joint Committee before the 3rd Meeting in 2011. Although the clear ambition of both sides is to make this an annual meeting, scheduling issues and other priorities have ensured that this dialogue has become a biannual event instead.

2019 (De & Pan, 2017; OEC, 2021). Whilst the value of trade is heavily skewed in favour of India, with approximately US$34.5 million, or 93%, of the trade coming from Indian exports to Mongolia, much of this trade involves finished industrial goods destined for Mongolia's mines (OEC, 2021). Furthermore, India's extended a US$1 billion line of credit to Mongolia in 2015 for the purposes of establishing the country's first oil refinery so it can diminish its dependence on energy from Russia. This loan was expanded by a further US$236 million in 2019, although construction has been delated by the COVID-19 pandemic (MEA, 2021). India has also been keen to provide Mongolia aid, most notably drawing on its strong pharmaceutical industry to provide Mongolia with medical supplies and vaccines both before and during the COVID-19 pandemic (Bayasgalan & Jargalsaikhan, 2021).

The Geopolitics behind Indo-Mongolia's Growing Convergence

To a large extent, the recent growth of Indo-Mongolian relations does represent the evolution of the early efforts in the post-Cold War era to cultivate good relations. However, there have also been an increasing convergence of interests derived from three interlinked factors that have propelled bilateral relations forward since 2010: first, India's emergence in earnest as a rising great power; second, Mongolia's mining boom from the mid-2000s; and finally, a mutual desire to find alternatives to China's increasingly overbearing behaviour in the region.

India has long maintained the pretence of being a great power, seeking to adopt the mantle of global leadership in several multilateral organisations such as the Non-Aligned Movement and often attempting to assert itself as the hegemon of South Asia. Indeed, a significant motivating factor behind India's Look East and Look North policies was to gain influence and augment its capabilities within Asia (Ganguly & Pardesi, 2009, pp. 13–14; Kavalski, 2015, pp. 428–430). However, for the first fifty to sixty years of India's independence, few states outside of its immediate local region took note or considered India to be a serious alternative to other powers such as China, Europe and the USA. It was only in the late 2000s did India's economic growth start to make significant strides and its and military procurement and diplomatic efforts began to bear fruit. Hence, India was able to establish itself as a bonified rising power, recognised as such through the BRICs minilateral grouping of states and increasingly able to match its claims with actions (Takenori, 2017). As a consequence of India's newly developed capabilities, its potential for regional leadership and partnership have been taken more seriously by the host of minor powers in Asia, including Mongolia.

Whilst India's growth as a rising power attracted Mongolia's gaze, India became increasingly interested in the potential Mongolia as a source of resources to help drive its continued growth. After the Mongolia passed a number of reforms incentivising foreign investment into its resource sector in the late-2000s, its mining sector boomed between 2009 and 2014, attracting many workers away from the traditional animal husbandry and textile industries (Dai & Gibson, 2012, pp. 3–4; Muller, 2019). Whilst the resource sector saw a global downturn when commodity price fell in 2014-2015, the industry has since rebounded and Mongolia's mines have continued to dominate its economy. Although economic statistics indicate that Mongolia primary export to India is still wool and hides (OEC, 2021), India has shown great interest in procuring coking coal, uranium and copper as well as investing in Mongolia's energy sector (Bayasgalan & Jargalsaikhan, 2021, pp. 4–6; De & Pan, 2017, pp. 36–38). Indeed, the largest line of credit that India has extended to any country, specifically US$1.2 billion, has been to develop the first oil refinery in Mongolia and both sides evidently keen to expand Indian investment and trade in Mongolia's resource sector (MEA, 2019). With construction work only recently started on the refinery, it will remain to be seen to what extent this help open up opportunities for the export of mineral resources to India in the future.

Whilst India's rise and Mongolia's mineral wealth have increased the two state's mutual interest in each other, it is their shared concern over China's increasingly assertive behaviour that is arguably the most significant factor propelling bilateral engagements. Throughout the 2010s, India's relations with China deteriorated as confrontations along their shared border became increasingly common and violent, culminating in the lethal skirmish in the Galwan Valley in 2020. Additionally, India has been increasingly concerned with China's increasing efforts to establish Belt and Road projects throughout the Indian Ocean region, including the China-Pakistan Economic Corridor (Boon, 2016; Deepak, 2020). For its part, Mongolia has been evidently uneasy about the growth of Chinese influence over it. This concern has stemmed not only due to its established policy of avoiding becoming dependent on any one state but also due to China's willingness to use coercion in response to policies it disapproves of. The most notable instance of this occurred when China briefly shut its border with Mongolia in 2002 in response to a visit from the Dalai Lama, temporarily crippling Mongolian trade (Reeves, 2012, p. 594). Hence, Mongolia has been seeking options since the late to dilute and/or curtail Chinese presence and influence without destroying their economy.

However, openly attempting to balance against China is not an option for either state. An actual alliance would be infeasible given the distance between the two states. Despite the tensions, China represents India's largest trading partner, with bilateral trade between the two expected to reach US$100 billion in 2021 with Indian exports improving (Jayaswal, 2021). Additionally, India works alongside China in several multilateral organisations such as the Asian Infrastructure Development Bank, the BRICS summit and the Shanghai Cooperation Organisation. For Mongolia, the issues are even starker. Approximately 70 percent of Mongolian trade is with China and Chinese ports such as Tianjin acting as the main import/export rout for trade with the rest of the world (Soni, 2020, p. 70). Furthermore, the sheer geographic distance ensures that any moves to form an alliance or even engage in *de facto* balancing actions would be unfeasible, likely attracting China's wrath whilst remaining difficult for either party to fulfil any commitments to deter reprisals. Thus, India and Mongolia have opted for a milder version of balancing known as 'hedging'.

In essence, hedging form of strategic alignment behaviour in which a state seeks to keep its position towards the centres of power ambiguous and open, neither seeking to 'bandwagon' with or balance against one power or the other (Kuik, 2016; Lim & Cooper, 2015). This is typically achieved through a 'engage and resist strategy', in which a state mixes both cooperation and counteraction policies as a contingency plan with the aim of minimising risk whilst and maximising benefits (Korolev, 2019, p. 422). It is important to note that hedging is a contested term in the theoretical scholarly literature.[6] Nonetheless, Indo-Mongolian relations clearly have a strong undertone of mutual assistance to resist domination by China whilst remaining well below the threshold that could generate legitimate concern or potential reprises from the penultimate global power.

Specifically, India has been recognised by several scholars as attempting to maintain its strategic autonomy via a strategy of 'multi-alignment' (Hall, 2016). This has seen India cooperating with China at an international level in breaking down the unipolar world whilst resisting China at a regional and/or local level through the development of strategic partnerships and independent capabilities (Boon, 2016, pp. 795–799; Takenori, 2017, pp. 475–479). Similarly, Mongolia's foreign policy after 2010 has followed what scholar Jeffery Reeves (2012) has identified as blend of 'omni-enmeshment' and 'complex balancing of influence'. In essence, this has effectively seen Mongolia seek to embrace as many prominent international partners and multilateral organisations as possible in order to curb Chinese (and to a lesser extent Russian) influence without provoking any retribution or getting unintentionally drawn into an alliance or becoming dependent on another overmighty patron (Soni, 2020). Thus, both India and Mongolia appear to have found in each other the perfect partner to help enhance their capabilities and limit Chinese influence without committing to an alliance or overtly directing their cooperation against China.

6 Specifically, the debate largely revolves around whether hedging should be considered a distinct activity or a form of balancing behaviour. There are also debates about whether hedging is a common option or a 'luxury' for some states, under what circumstances will states choose to hedge over balancing/band wagoning/attempting isolation etc.

Conclusion

Although diplomatic and other engagements between India and Mongolia prior to 2010 were negligible, the decade between 2010 and 2020 has seen a palpable expansion of bilateral relations. The scope and frequency of diplomatic, defence, development and political dialogues has increased and both states seem to be keen on exploring how the relationship can be furthered (MEA, 2019). Naturally, this relationship has been built upon the inroads created in the 1990s and 2000s, but it was a convergence of three key factors that have brought India and Mongolia into close communication. First has been the emergence of India as a bonafide regional power, able to appear as an attractive market and partner to minor powers within Asia. Second was the growth of Mongolia's resource sector, with resource extraction quickly dominating its economic output and attracting many foreign investors. Finally, and potentially most importantly, both India and Mongolia had a shared desire to hedge against China's rise, seeking to strengthen their capabilities and partnerships to resist any attempts as coercion whilst still maintaining as friendly relations with their largest trading partner.

Nonetheless, it should not be forgotten that there are still major obstacles in the two states developing a genuinely productive partnership. China and Russia still dominate Mongolia's economic and strategic engagement, with its engagement with other third neighbour partners such as the USA, Japan and South Korea often eclipsing India's (Campi, 2018). India for its part remains focused on its immediate neighbourhood and great power politics, frequently distracted by confrontations along its borders with Pakistan and China as well as developing its relationships such as the Quad. Mongolia's landlocked position also renders active engagement and trade between the two states difficult. Hence, even an optimistic Indian brief on Indo-Mongolian relations conceded that, despite the numerous talks and investment initiatives, bilateral trade remains "modest in value and volume" (MEA, 2021).

Ultimately, the current Indo-Mongolian relations can be best characterised as having plenty of bonhomie and potential, especially in terms of trade, but one that should not be overhyped. The sheer distance and more pressing matters may yet stymie further developments or even ensure that Indo-Mongolian relations wither. Yet the geopolitical factors that have brought the two states together are unlikely to shift any time soon. Thus, it can be expected that the confluence of interests between India and Mongolia will keep the states within each other's sight and ensuring that the bilateral relationship will have some ways yet to develop before it has reached its natural limits.

Acknowledgements:

This paper was originally presented at the 'India-Mongolia Relations: Beyond

Greater Central Asia' Seminar held in July 2021. The author would like to thank Dr. R. Srinivasan for the invitation and my fellow panellists, especially Dr. Sureyya Yigit, for the discussion and ideas that helped me refine my argumentation.

References:

Acharya, A. (2015). India's 'Look East' Policy. In D. M. Malone, C. R. Mohan, & S. Raghavan (Eds.), *The Oxford Handbook on Indian Foreign Policy* (pp. 452–465).

Bajpaee, C. (2017). Dephasing India's Look East/Act East Policy. *Contemporary Southeast Asia, 39*(2), 348–372. https://doi.org/10.1355/cs39-2d

Batbayar, T. (2001). Mongolia, New Central Asia and India. *Himalayan and Central Asian Studies, 5*(1), 67–79. https://www-proquest-com.libproxy.murdoch.edu.au/docview/1325025320/A0918218625147 39PQ/10?accountid=12629

Bayasgalan, N., & Jargalsaikhan, M. (2021). *Why are India and Mongolia strategic partners?* (No. 8; Mongolian Geopolitics). Friedrich Ebert Stiftung. http://library.fes.de/pdf-files/bueros/mongolei/17932.pdf

Boon, H. T. (2016). The hedging prong in India's evolving China strategy. *Journal of Contemporary China, 25*(101), 792–804. https://doi.org/10.180/10670564.2016.1160527

Campi, A. (2018). Mongolian Foreign Relations under 25 Years of Democracy. In T.-K. Chang & A. Chang (Eds.), *Routledge Handbook of Asia in World Affairs* (pp. 61–104). Routledge.

Chandramohan, B. (2015, June 15). India and Mongolia: Uranium and Beyond [News and analysis]. *Future Directions International.* https://www.futuredirections.org.au/publication/india-and-mongolia-uranium-and-beyond/

Dai, C. H., & Gibson, D. T. (2012). *Minegolia: Part 1, China and Mongolia's Mining Boom.* The Wilson Center. https://www.wilsoncenter.org/publication/minegolia-part-i-china-and-mongolias-mining-boom

De, P., & Pan, S. (2017). India-Mongolia Economic Relations: Current Status and Future Prospect. *The Northeast Asian Economic Review, 5*(2), 31–47.

Deepak, B. R. (2020). *India and China: Beyond the Binary of Friendship and Enmity.* Springer.

Defence News India. (2019, October 3). India Mongolia conduct Nomadic Elephant military exercise. *Defence Star.* https://www.defencestar.in/diplomacy-news/india-defence-news-indian-army-india-mongolia-conduct-joint-military-exercise-nomadic-elephant/2473/

Ganapathi, M. (2015). 'Look East—Act East' Dimension of Indian Foreign Policy. *Indian Foreign Affairs Journal, 10*(1), 63–73.

Ganguly, S., & Pardesi, M. S. (2009). Explaining Sixty Years of India's Foreign Policy. *India Review, 8*(1), 4–19. https://doi.org/10.1080/14736480802665162

Hall, I. (2016). Multialignment and Indian Foreign Policy under Narendra Modi. *The Round Table, 105*(3), 271–286. https://doi.org/10.1080/00358533.2016.1180760

Jayaswal, R. (2021, October 19). Despite Galwan, India's trade with China has grown. But there is a shift. *Hindustan Times.* https://www.hindustantimes.com/analysis/despite-galwan-india-s-trade-with-china-has-grown-but-there-is-a-shift-101634624617348.html

Kaplonski, C. (2004). *Truth, History and Politics in Mongolia: The Memory of Heroes.* RoutledgeCurzon.

Kavalski, E. (2010). *India and Central Asia: The Mythmaking and International Relations of a Rising Power.* I.B.Tauris & Co. Ltd.

Kavalski, E. (2015). India's Bifurcated Look to 'Central Eurasia': The Central Asian Republics and Afghanistan. In D. M. Malone, C. R. Mohan, & S. Raghavan (Eds.), *The Oxford Handbook of Indian Foreign Policy* (pp. 424–436). Oxford University Press.

Korolev, A. (2019). Shrinking room for hedging: System-unit dynamics and behavior of smaller power. *International Relations of the Asia-Pacific, 19*(3), 419–452. https://doi.org/10.1093/irap/lcz011

Krishna, V. (2020). India and its Extended Neighbourhood: Engagements with Mongolia and Central Asia. *The Mongolian Journal of International Affairs, 21*, 101–115.

Kuik, C.-C. (2016). How do weaker states hedge? Unpacking ASEAN states' alignment behaviour towards China. *Journal of Contemporary China, 25*(100), 500–514. https://doi.org/10.1080/10670564.2015.1132714

Lim, D. J., & Cooper, Z. (2015). Reassessing Hedging: The Logic of Alignment in East Asia. *Security Studies, 24*(4), 696–727. https://doi.org/10.1080/09636412.1103130

MEA, (Ministry of External Affairs). (2001). *Joint Declaration.* Ministry of External Affairs, Government of India. https://mea.gov.in/Speeches-Statements.htm?dtl/5524/Joint+Declaration

MEA, (Ministry of External Affairs). (2015). *Joint Statement for India-Mongolia Strategic Partnership.* Ministry of External Affairs, Government of India. https://www.mea.gov.in/outoging-visit-detail.htm?25253/Joint+Statement+for+IndiaMongolia+Strategic+Partnership+May+17+2015

MEA, (Ministry of External Affairs). (2019). *Joint Statement on Strengthening the Strategic Partnership between Mongolia and India.* Government of India Press. https://www.mea.gov.in/bilateral-documents.htm?dtl/31841/Joint_Statement_on_Strengthening_the_Strategic_

MEA, (Ministry of External Affairs). (2020). *7th Meeting of India-Mongolia Joint Committee on Cooperation.* Ministry of External Affairs, Government of India. https://www.mea.gov.in/press-releases.htm?dtl/33256/7th+Meeting+of+IndiaMongolia+Joint+Committee+on+Cooperation

MEA, (Ministry of External Affairs). (2021). *Brief on India-Mongolia Bilateral Relations.* Government of India Press. https://eoi.gov.in/ulaanbaatar/?pdf4346?000

MFA, (Ministry of Foreign Affairs). (n.d.). *National Security Concept of Mongolia.* Ministry of Foreign Affairs, Mongolia. https://mfa.gov.mn/en/documentation/55280/

MJIA, (The Editors of The Mongolian Journal of International Affairs). (1995). Documents: Concept of Mongolia's Foreign Policy. *The Mongolian Journal of International Affairs, 2,* 56–63. file:///C:/Users/20096702/Downloads/439-Article%20Text-1681-1-10-20150501%20(1).pdf

Muller, N. (2019, October 22). Mongolia's New Mining Boom. *The Diplomat.* https://thediplomat.com/2019/10/mongolias-new-mining-boom/

Narangoa, L. (2009). Mongolia and Preventive Diplomacy: Haunted by History and Becoming Cosmopolitan. *Asian Survey, 49*(2), 358–379.

OEC, (Observatory of Economic Complexity). (2021). *India / Mongolia trade data.* https://oec.world/en/profile/bilateral-country/ind/partner/mng?depthSelector=HS-2Depth&dynamicBilateralTradeSelector=year2019&measureBilateralTradeSelector=vizValueOption1

PTI, (Press Trust of India). (2018, February 13). Mongolian border force team being trained by BSF. *Outlook.* https://www.outlookindia.com/newsscroll/mongolian-border-force-team-being-trained-by-bsf/1252353

Reeves, J. (2012). Mongolia's evolving security strategy: Omnienmeshment and balance of influence. *The Pacific Review, 25*(5), 589–612. https://doi.org/10.1080/09512748.2012.728241

Sikri, R. (2009). India's 'Look East' Policy. *Asia-Pacific Review, 16*(1), 131–145. https://doi.org/10.1080/13439000902957624

Soni, S. K. (2015). The 'Third Neighbour' Approach of Mongolia's Diplomacy of External Relations: Effects on Relations between India and Mongolia. *India Quarterly, 71*(1), 37–52.

Soni, S. K. (2016). Emerging Dimensions of India-Mongolia Relations. *Indian Foreign Affairs Journal, 11*(1), 51–62.

Soni, S. K. (2020). Turning Points in Mongolian Policy of External Engagement: Expediency and Outcomes. *The Mongolian Journal of International Affairs, 21,* 64–78. https://doi.org/10.5564/mjia.v21i0.1434

Takenori, H. (2017). Explaining India's Foreign Policy: From Dream to Realization of Major Power. *International Relations of the Asia-Pacific, 17*(2), 463–496. https://doi.org/10.1093/irap/lcx)11

Wani, A. (2020). *India and China in Central Asia: Understanding the new rivalry in the heart of Eurasia* (ORF Occasional Papers No. 235; p. 38). Observer Research Foundation. https://www.orfonline.org/wp-content/uploads/2020/02/ORF_OccasionalPaper_235_India-China-CAR_NEW-19Feb.pdf

2. Mongolia's Historic Relations with its Largest Neighbour: Russia

Sureyya Yigit, PhD[1]

Abstract

Mongolia's foreign policy can be seen as fairly straightforward given the fact it has only two neighbours. The only problem is, however, the neighbours are Russia and China. This is a challenge that Mongolians have been facing for centuries and especially so since gaining their independence in the 20th century as the world's second socialist state. This article examines the origins of the Mongol-Russian relationship, noting the geopolitical importance of Mongolian territories both for Czarist Russia and the Bolshevik Revolution. It investigates the twists and turns that have endured throughout this relationship, offering an insight into the very recent past as well as the present.

Keywords: Mongolia, Russia, Geopolitics, Foreign Policy, Northeast Asia, Cross-border Trade, Strategy

Introduction

Russia has always been a close neighbour throughout Mongolian history. Equally, Mongolia occupies a special place in Russia's relations with the countries of the East. Early relations between Russia and Mongolia were established in the 17th century, which developed further incrementally, with a unique role played by Russia in the formation of an independent Mongolian state in the 20th century. Russia primarily provided diplomatic support, military and economic assistance.

An essential factor in terms of the national security of Mongolia has been its relations with two large neighbouring countries -Russia and China. The nature of

1 Dr Sureyya Yigit is Professor of Politics and International Relations, School of Politics and Diplomacy, New Vision University, Tbilisi, Georgia.

this relationship can be identified in the shape of a triangle: Russia - Mongolia - China, each especially being one of the corners throughout the twentieth century. The international position of Mongolia changed radically several times during this century depending on the balance of power in East Asia, from either a strengthening or weakening of China or Russia. Until 1911 Mongolia was part of the Qing Empire, after which the influence of Russia was decisive. From the middle of the nineteenth century, one can notice a gradual strengthening of the role of Russia in this region, whereby Russian-Mongolian trade began to expand and the Russian consulate in Urga began to operate and increase its influence.[1]

The Chinese Revolution, and related to this, national liberation, are significant developments for the Mongolian people, who in 1911 achieved the creation of an independent state for Mongolia, which was determined to engage in the newly emerging international situation in the region. The declaration by Mongolia in December 1911 to secede from the Qing Empire and appeal to the Czarist Empire for support and assistance in the formation of an independent state lead quite understandably to a strengthening of Russia's position.[2] During 1911-1915 Russian-Mongolian relations developed further and became closer, although this period was also characterised by an intense confrontation between Mongolia's two neighbouring powers.[3]

With the balance of power between Russia and China in flux, economic aid by Russia enabled Mongolia to conduct a series of economic and military reforms. The Kyakha tripartite conference of 1915 defined the status of Mongolia as an autonomous state within Republican China.[4] The First World War, followed by the Russian revolutions of 1917, significantly weakened the role of Russia in North-East Asia in general and Mongolia in particular. By 1919, the actual independence of Mongolia was abolished by the introduction of White forces to the nomadic country; thus, the international balance of power was upset, and China became increasingly significant alongside a rising and influential Japan.

In 1921, as a result of the national democratic revolution, national independence restored the initial independence of Mongolia, after which it implemented radical revolutions transforming its society and bringing it under significant influence of the Comintern and Soviet Russia, effectively becoming a "satellite" of the USSR.[5] Thus, a small nomadic country came to be dependent on its two giant neighbours. A weakening of one of them, the exacerbation of internal problems and decentralisation processes led to strengthening the role of the northern neighbour. The Soviets held a deep revolutionary interest in all its neighbours, primarily focusing on military-strategic and economic interests within Asia. The favourable geographic position of Mongolia located in the centre of the Asian continent, the vast territory and the presence of numerous livestock as a source of agricultural raw materials for Siberia and central Russia made it highly attractive to cooperate with both in terms of trade and the military-strategic sphere.

The serious interest of the Russians in Mongolia was also determined by the unique historic role of the Mongols of the 13th – 15th centuries, namely the Mongol-Tatar invasion of Russia, the composition of the Golden Horde.[6] Due to its nature and resources and the events taking place both internally and within its vicinity, Mongolia became a topic that attracted the constant attention of Russia. As diplomatic relations between Russia and Mongolia began, an increase in the size of Russian-Mongolian trade also enticed greater Russian interest in Mongolia's economy and society. In 1861 a Russian consulate was established in Urga, and with the Russian-Chinese Treaty of 1881, Russia received the right of duty-free trade throughout Mongolia.[7] Commercial activity further developed with Russian merchants, and trading companies began to establish businesses. In 1895, the Russian-Chinese Bank was established in St. Petersburg, and in 1900 branches of this bank had opened in Urga and Ulyasutai.[8] More Russian consulates were opened in Ulyasutai, Kobdo, Maymachen.[9] This period witnessed not only the exports of Russian goods to Mongolia but also capital. Russian entrepreneurs in Urga created small factories, and a joint-stock company was organised, mining and prospecting for gold in Mongolia.[10]

In Russia, by the end of the nineteenth century, a change in foreign policy concerning defensive policy in the Far East and Central Asia began to take place, which foresaw a more active, offensive dimension. The development of industry, economic development of the Urals, Siberia and the Far East stimulated modern infrastructure. In 1891, with the construction of the Trans-Siberian railway accessed for Russian traders and business circles, the markets of the countries of East Asia.[11] The conclusion with Qing China of a contract for the construction of the Chinese Eastern Railway, a lease for 25 years of a military base in Port Arthur testified to the strengthening of the position of Russia in the Far East.[12]

Therefore, at the beginning of the twentieth century, Russian diplomacy was faced with a difficult task: to ensure the defence of the national interests of Russia, but without drawing it into military conflicts. The weakening of the Qing Empire became an arena of rivalry between the great European powers such as the United States, Britain, Germany, France, and Russia. The results of the Sino-Japanese War of 1894-1895, Russian-Japanese War 1904-1905 demonstrated that the region included a rising new strong power: Japan. According to the Russian-Japanese Agreement of 1907, the Japanese government recognised special interests in Outer Mongolia.[13] Russia, in turn, recognised the Japanese interests concerning southern Manchuria and Inner Mongolia, as well as a Japanese protectorate in Korea.

Since the beginning of the 20th century, the Qing government of China had strengthened its colonisation of Mongol lands complemented by the military, administrative and trading expansion. Incrementally the occupation of border Mongol territories began with Chinese merchants leading the penetration, who quickly took over the Mongolian market.[14] For the Chinese, the colonist was primarily a Chinese official administrator and a Chinese soldier. Russia's policy was determined by an interest in the Mongolian trading opportunities, expanding Russian interests, establishing a presence against possible Japanese aggression, and Chinese capital's economic pressure. Russian capital and Siberian merchants were also attracted to the Mongolian market, specifically interested in cheap Mongolian raw materials such as wool, leather and meat, as well as lucrative opportunities to export their industrial products.[15]

On the Mongolian market, greater competition was generated by Western industrial goods, which Chinese traders sold. The dynamic development of the Russian economy at the end of the nineteenth and early twentieth centuries allowed more significant support for education, culture and science. Improving the educational system and the development of science led to significant scientific and technical developments. Russia supported geographical research focusing on Central Asia, notably through Przhevalsky, Roborovsky, Potanin and Kozlov.[16] The establishment and activity of the Imperial Geographical Society and its branches in Siberia contributed to the scientific research on Mongolia.[17] The events that took place in Mongolia during the restoration of national independence and related changes in Russian-Mongolian relations, discussion and preparation of the Russian-Chinese trade agreement in 1911 led to an unprecedented interest in Mongolia in the most diverse strata of Russian society.[18]

Interest in Russia, however, acquired a more practical direction associated with Mongolia. Various members of the Russian elite: political and military leaders, representatives of diplomacy, academics and commercial circles, journalists and scholars investigated the various characteristics of the state of the Russian-Mongolian relationships. In specific ways in socio-political thought, Russia formulated a "Mongolian question".[19] Mongolia's direct appeal to the Russian Empire for diplomatic support and economic assistance and the arrival of the Mongolian delegation to St. Petersburg forced the Czarist elite, primarily Russian government circles and representatives of various political parties, to determine what their attitude to the "Mongolian issue" was. According to some, Mongolia needed to be tied to Russia and transformed into a colony.[20] Others suggested creating a buffer state which would be dependent on Russia.[21] Still, others believed it was a mistake to interfere in the internal affairs of Mongolia and believed in the necessity of creating an independent Mongolian state.[22] In Russia, social and political thought reflected the entire spectrum of ideological views, party political directions, including the Octobrists, Cadets, Monarchists and Social Democrats.[23]

Quite naturally, the "Mongolian question" was not the main external political issue for the public throughout the empire which was embroiled in complex international relations both in the West and East. However, the Mongolian question as an integral part of Far Eastern policy and relations with China increased the importance of Mongolia, especially with regard to bilateral trading relations. Perhaps throughout the entire century since then, there has never been such a deep and wide interest within Russian socio-political thought concerning the Mongolian question, as at the beginning of the twentieth century, especially after 1911. This period witnessed a conspicuous surge in the release of literature on Mongolia, Russian-Mongolian-Chinese relations, and perspectives on how to develop these relationships.[24]

Thus, the formation of Russian-Mongolian relations at the beginning of the 20th century took place in a complex system of international relations in East Asia, in the system of relations between China, Russia, Japan and Mongolia. During this period, there was a manifest increase in attention towards Outer Mongolia from China and Russia, fueled by the inevitable trading rivalry between Russian and Chinese merchants. The deterrence factor of Russia in Mongolia could be seen through the obligations made under the Russian-Japanese agreements of 1907, 1910 and 1912, which defined the spheres of influence in the region.[25] The increasingly complicated international situation around Mongolia stimulated widespread discussion of the Mongolian question in the government circles of Russia and the pages of scientific and periodicals.[26] This was significantly intensified in connection with the revision of the Russian-Chinese trade agreements in 1911 and the proclamation of Outer Mongolia in December 1911 of its political independence. The "Mongolian question" came to be discussed in the Russian State Duma with several major Meetings held in St. Petersburg, Moscow and Irkutsk to study the Mongolian market, organising several trade expeditions to Mongolia.[27]

The formulation of Russia's policy concerning Mongolia took place in the struggle and compromise of various tendencies determined by political forces and leading departments, namely the Ministry of Foreign Affairs, the Ministry of Finance and the military.[28] Foreign policy in the empire was determined by attempts to resolve the emerging contradictions between the diplomatic department and trade industrial circles, between central and regional administration, various levels of local administration, and representatives of the military department. Thus, in the discussion of Russian-Mongolian relations and the "Mongolian question", the following main directions can be identified: assessments of diplomats and statesmen of Russia, characteristics of military specialists, representatives of commerce and industry, academics and the intelligentsia.[29]

Analysis of the assessments of Russian diplomats such as Foreign Minister

Sazonov on the "Mongolian Question", a series of Russian-Mongolian-Chinese agreements during 1911-1915 suggested a strict and restrained diplomatic line to be pursued by Russia in Mongolia.[30] Russia strove to maintain peaceful relations with Republican China, fulfil the secret points of the Russian-Japanese agreements on the delimitation of spheres of influence, and support the independence of the development of Outer Mongolia.[31] Russia could not support the complete independence of Outer Mongolia with the annexation of Inner Mongolia.[32] Russian diplomacy directed all its efforts to create an autonomous Mongolia and recognise Russia's special rights in Outer Mongolia. Russia was in a difficult situation since, on the one hand, she needed to limit the aspirations of the Mongols to create a "Greater Mongolia" and, on the other side, persuade China to make concessions, show flexibility and recognise the autonomy of Mongolia.[33] Thanks to a flexible policy, diplomats managed to create an autonomous, and in fact, independent Mongolia. During 1910-1916 Foreign Minister Sazonov considered Russia a European power with active external politics in Europe and the Middle East and opposed increasing Russian possessions in Asia.[34]

At a meeting of the State Duma on April 13-27, 1912, polar points of view on the problem of the prospects for Russian-Mongolian relations were evident.[35] Sazonov and Milyukov advocated only for a mediating role between Mongolia and China and against involvement in internal activities of Mongolian affairs, whereas others considered it necessary to annex Mongolia to Russia.[36] Sazonov opposed the complete separation of Mongolia from China, considering it not ready for independent political development, which would also burden Russia to create a viable state with corresponding financial obligations, time, and effort.[37]

Sazonov did not consider the annexation of Mongolia to Russia a valuable acquisition, as it could lead to an undesirable significant shift in the centre of gravity within the state and, accordingly, to the weakening of Russia's positions in Europe and the Middle East. To not be drawn too deeply into the East and Mongol affairs, it was best for Russia to undertake the role of a mediator. Opposing views centred on the belief that Mongolia should become a buffer state that would cover the eastern borders of Russia.[38] Emperor Nicholas II also influenced the practical solution of the "Mongolian question" with his preference for imperial territorial expansion.[39]

In this respect, a special place in the study of Russian-Mongolian relations was reserved for military analyses. Mongolia and Northeastern China were studied as possible theatres of military operations, the military potential of neighbouring states. They possessed valuable scientific information about the country, received during unique expeditions, and critical analysis of scientific literature about Mongolia, detailing information concerning cities, history, climate, religion, and trade and transport routes.[40]

The military focused on the threat to Russia from China and Japan coming from the East, threatening the tranquillity of Russia and Europe, believing it to carry the seeds of destruction of European civilisation and culture. Since the beginning of the twentieth century, active colonisation in Manchuria and Mongolia took place through Chinese and Japanese railroad construction projects and roads.[41] Moreover, the modernisation of Chinese troops was testified by the opinions of the military concerning the threat of the invasion of China and Japan in the Siberian region. Therefore, helping the Mongols build their autonomous state, relocating the Russian army to the edge of the Gobi desert would create a buffer zone and avoid a military collision with China. The results of the General Staff research became a valuable source of information about Mongolia, and their influence was very significant, although not decisive. They fueled the direction in foreign policy of taking an active hard stance in this region.[42] While there is a possibility that army specialists somewhat exaggerated the military threat posed by China in favour of a strict policy towards this eastern neighbour, they alerted Russia to a relationship fraught with military conflicts and diplomatic complications. At the initial outset, it was Russian-Mongolian trade relations which played a prominent role in relations between the two countries.[43]

The forecasted increase in Russian exports to Mongolia not being realized caused anxiety among the commercial and industrial circles of central Russia. In 1909 and 1910, at the Moscow Exchange Committee, meetings of Moscow industrialists were held, which discussed the problems of trade with China and Mongolia. Essential roles in the study of Russian-Mongolian trade were the two trade expeditions to Mongolia: One was Moscow led with Colonel Popov, equipped with industrialists, another was a Siberian expedition from Tomsk.[44] The approaches of these two expeditions to the problem and their conclusions differed significantly.[45] The Moscow trade expedition recognised the importance of the Mongolian market for Russia, although it could not foresee many prospects of Russian trade in Mongolia.[46] The businessmen and traders of central Russia saw their economic interests tied more closely with the further developed markets of the Middle East and Manchuria.

The Siberian expedition, headed by professors Bogolev and Sobolev, gave a more profound economic analysis of the state of Russian-Mongolian trade.[47] They considered Mongolia a promising market for Russian goods; therefore, it was far better to strengthen the Russians' trading positions.[48] Representatives of the intelligentsia suggested a different interpretation of the situation from the military and merchants concerning Mongolia. They also encouraged the creation of an independent Mongolia, a buffer state which would become a part of a union of European states. These views were reflected in the publication of leading Mongolologists of Russia such as the liberal populist Popov, linguist and ethnographer Evstafiev, official and local historian Pershin, the future the famous Mongolian scholar Burdukov, and a graduate of the Eastern Institute in Vladivostok, Bobrik.[49] Despite the difference in details, they advocated the creation of an independent Mongolian state or buffer state.

They advocated for Russia to provide genuine assistance to Mongolia. As vital to reviving the Mongolian state, they considered supporting the establishment of the economy of the Mongolian nomads, assisting in the further development of trade relations.[50] Particular attention should be focused on the need for assistance in the field of cultural and health care.[51] The Social Democrats occupied a particular position in the "Mongolian question". They based their position on class positions, on criticism of the colonial and conquest policies of the Tsarist government in the backward countries of the East, including in Mongolia.[52] The Social Democrats did not show tremendous and deep interest in Mongolia and the policy of Russia in the region. The absence of a working class in the country, the insignificant Mongolian role in the world economy and politics, and weak awareness of events in a nomadic country became important pointers concerning the characteristics and assessments of the "Mongolian question". Moreover, it was only the Chinese Revolution and the aggravation of Mongolia-Chinese relations increased their interest in this problem. In terms of historiography, the Bolsheviks quickly and calmly turned Mongolia into a zone of influence and spreading revolutionary ideas.[53]

At the end of World War II, the Union of Soviet Socialist States (USSR), as a victorious party, achieved the international recognition of Mongolia, which became a loyal ally for the entire period of the Cold War, supporting all its initiatives in the international arena.[54] After the collapse of the USSR, the new Russian leadership warmed much more to the West in expectation of more profitable foreign economic partners. With the socialist system collapsing rapidly, Mongolia, experiencing many internal problems in its socio-economic and political life, found itself without the support of its long-term ally. Relations between Mongolia and Russia entered a stagnation period and culminated in the near curtailment of bilateral contacts.

This state of bilateral relations lasted for around a decade, during which significant changes took place in Mongolia itself, especially concerning its foreign policy. The Mongolian leadership overcame the negative socio-economic trends and political obstacles and demonstrated the ability to move forward both in domestic and foreign policy, as a result of which a new type of Mongolian statehood arose. In 1992, Mongolia adopted a new Constitution, which laid down the legal foundations for a new political system and market economy; and a multi-party system was finally proclaimed.[55]

In its Preamble and first Article, the Constitution declared:[56]

We, the people of Mongolia:

- consolidating and strengthening the independence and sovereignty of our state,
- respecting and upholding the human rights and freedom, justice, and unity of our nation,
- inheriting and cherishing the traditions of our statehood, history and culture,
- considering and respecting the accomplishments of human civilisation,
- shall aspire to the supreme goal of building and developing a humane, civic and democratic society in our motherland.

Thus, do hereby proclaim and declare this Constitution of Mongolia to the entire populace.

Article 1

1. Mongolia is an independent and sovereign Republic.
2. Securing democracy, justice, freedom, equality, national unity and respecting the rule of law are the fundamental principles of the State activities.

Therefore, according to this Constitution, Mongolia is an independent, sovereign state based on the principles of democracy, justice, freedom, equality, ensuring national harmony, and respect for the law. Thus, a new Mongolia began to build relations with other states, not on an ideological basis but an equal, mutually beneficial basis.

Mongolia began to integrate into the new system of international relations and the world economy while possessing a vast and rich reserve of natural resources; hence it came as no surprise to witness that Mongolia did not remain alone for long. Western companies flocked to Mongolia, offering lucrative contracts and investments in the development of Mongolian natural resources.[57] At the turn of the 21st century, Mongolia's standing in international relations had increased dramatically. Equally, Russia once again realised the significance of Mongolia and began to turn eastward and limit the missed political and economic gains from having loosened relations with its recent rally.

With the election of Vladimir Putin as President of Russia in 2000, Russia set out to strengthen the eastern vector of its foreign policy.[58] At the highest level, Russia began to make efforts to restore its relations with Ulaanbaatar. Nevertheless, it was not easy to return to the previous state of relations, since in a short time, Mongolia had established a beneficial cooperative relationship with China, the USA,

South Korea, Turkey, Japan, Canada and other economically developed countries. The Russian Federation realised soon after that this country which occupied an important strategic position in the depths of Inner Asia, was turning into an arena of open and hidden political and economic rivalry between such actors as itself, China, the United States, Japan, the EU, Turkey, Great Britain, Canada, South Korea, and others.

The relevance of Mongolia and the pivot to the Pacific idea by Moscow was definitely affected by the continued advancement of NATO forces up to the borders of Russia and the continuation of Western economic sanctions.[59] This encouraged Russia to develop further cooperation with the countries of the Asia-Pacific Region (APR) in order to connect Siberia and the Far East to the economic and political integration processes of the APR.[60] In such a measure, Mongolia could become one of the strong points, a hub, particularly a transit country for the development of trade, economic, humanitarian, logistic, and energy cooperation with the rest of the APR countries.

It has been asserted that Mongolia, due to its possession of vast reserves of natural resources, requires Russian energy resources, which is extremely promising for Russia in terms of economic cooperation.[61] According to the World Bank, Mongolia's GDP grew by a phenomenal 17.3% a decade ago in 2011 and by 12.3% the very next year.[62] Although the next decade did not fulfil this promise as it included a slowdown in GDP growth rates, cooperation with Russia remained very promising for Mongolia. In the updated Foreign Policy Concept adopted in 2011, Mongolia adopted the principle of balanced relations with Russia and China as the basis of its foreign policy. It proclaimed the concept of a "third neighbour" represented by the United States, Japan, South Korea, Turkey and others as a guarantee of sovereignty.[63] The aforementioned countries remain active in the development of co-cooperation with Mongolia.

Table: 1 Mongolia's Exports 2019

	Trade (US$ Mil)	Partner share (%)
China	2,037	33.24
Russian Federation	1,730	28.23
Japan	585	9.56
USA	290	4.73

Source: World Bank (n.d.). Mongolia trade. Retrieved July 31, 2021, from https://wits.worldbank.org/countrysnapshot/en/MNG

At the same time, the Mongolian leadership understood the difficulties in maintaining a balance in relations both with neighbours on the one side and with economically developed and politically democratic states on the other. As shown in Table 1, Russia was no longer the most critical trading partner for Mongolia. For example, in terms of the total volume of foreign trade, China accounted for 88.88% in 2019 whereas Russia was 0.89%, the Chinese market as a whole amounting to $6,773 Million, whereas Russia being limited to $68 Million.[64] At the same time, there is reason to believe that Mongolia can build a mutually beneficial strategic partnership with Russia even in the current challenging conditions of building a new world order. Initiating a balanced development of bilateral relations, Russia could provide Mongolia with sizeable political and diplomatic support to further upkeep the Mongolian state and extend bilateral relations. One can assert that Russia, traditionally having strategic interests in Mongolia, is likely to make noteworthy efforts to keep Mongolia as an advantageous political and economic partner and reliable neighbour.

Bilateral relations began to decline in the early 1990s before the strategic partnership began in 2016.[65] Therefore, one must identify the factors that influenced their development and outline possible prospects. Initially, three stages can be distinguished in relations between Russia and Mongolia: the first stage from 1990-1993, which can be characterised as a period of decline; the second stage between 1993-1999 regarded as a period of partial recovery and stabilisation; the third stage from 2000 to the present is the development of good-neighbourly relations advancing onto a strategic partnership. Each of these stages was caused by both objective and subjective reasons and required scientific understanding to identify its content, problems, and prospects for restoring strong and good-neighbourly relations in the interests of both countries.

Initial Stage: Severe Decline

The first stage of relations from 1990-1993 was the most painful and sensitive for both countries. During this period, not only did both regimes collapse, but the whole socialist camp broke down, which led to the elites of both countries being determined to get rid of ideological filters and build international relations based on shared human values and mutual benefit. The early 1990s significantly undermined Russian-Mongolian relations. Such a development was due to the domestic political developments in both countries. As a result, there was a sharp decline in the intensity of Russian-Mongolian relations. This period was characterised by a decline in relations in all areas, especially in trade and economic and the cultural, scientific, military.[66] Not surprisingly, Moscow halted aid, which previously accounted for 37% subsidisation of the Mongolian annual budget.[67]

In February 1991, the Russian Socialist Federated Soviet Republic and the

Mongolian People's Republic signed a Declaration of Friendship and Good Neighbourly Cooperation, in which both sides proclaimed a mutual rejection of ideological approaches to issues of bilateral relations.[68] The signing of the declaration testified that the countries had abandoned the ideological component in their mutual relations, and from that time on, pragmatism and mutual benefit became the main pillars in the relations between the two countries. During 1991-1993 several intergovernmental agreements were signed, including an agreement on trade and economic cooperation, on the creation of the Mongolian-Russian intergovernmental commission on trade, economic, scientific and technical cooperation.[69] Throughout this period, Mongolia experienced a severe economic crisis, from which it was able to re-emerge thanks to the successful implementation of radical economic reforms and foreign donor assistance.[70]

Stage Two: Stabilisation

Nevertheless, under these conditions, a momentous event that affected bilateral relations was the official visit to Moscow in January 1993 of Mongolian President Ochirbat. The fundamental Treaty on Friendly Relations and Cooperation between the Russian Federation and Mongolia was signed.[71] According to this agreement, Mongolia and Russia agreed through Article 1 that the parties considered each other as friendly states and will be guided in their relations by the principles of respect for sovereignty and independence, sovereign equality, non-use of force or threat of force, inviolability of borders, territorial integrity, non-interference in internal affairs, respect for human rights and fundamental freedoms, equality and the right of peoples to dispose of their own destiny, conscientious fulfilment of obligations, good neighbourliness, partnership and cooperation.[72]

The new treaty replaced the 1966 Treaty of Friendship and Cooperation that had been in force earlier. It was a fundamentally new treaty built on new principles of relations. This new treaty foresaw a new model of genuinely equal cooperation between two neighbouring countries. It must be recalled that an essential factor that predetermined the conclusion of the 1993 Treaty was the withdrawal of Soviet troops from Mongolia, which, did in a certain sense, bring it out from under the Russian security umbrella, but at the same time allowed the improvement of relations with China and ability to act in the international arena with initiatives that were of particular importance for maintaining peace and security.[73] This agreement became the basis for the conclusion of all subsequent agreements in various fields and put bilateral relations on the path of stabilisation.

Over the next few years, several intergovernmental agreements were concluded, including those on military-technical cooperation, on border checkpoints, simplified communication across the Russian-Mongolian state border, on the protection and use of transboundary waters, on cultural and scientific cooperation, on the avoidance of double taxation concerning taxes on income and property, on the conditions of mutual trips of citizens, on cooperation in the field of geological exploration and development of subsoil.[74] The legal and regulatory framework began to gradually form and improve, creating other fertile grounds for cooperation.

By the second half of the 1990s, contacts at all levels had significantly expanded. In 1995, President Ochirbat took part in the celebrations in Moscow on the occasion of the 50th anniversary of Victory in the Great Patriotic War; in December 1999, the new President of Mongolia, Natsagiin Bagabandi, paid an official visit to Moscow; in 1999, a delegation of the Russian Federation Council headed by Varnavsky, head of the Russian Foreign Ministry Ivanov visited Mongolia, and in July 1999, his Mongolian colleague Nyam-Osoryn Tuyaa visited Russia.[75] During the second half of the 1990s, economic relations had significantly expanded and intensified.

Stage Three: Recovery

The third stage was essentially a turning point in relations between Mongolia and Russia, during which good-neighbourly relations began to develop into strategic ones, which was assisted by the election in March 2000 of Vladimir Putin as President of the Russian Federation.[76] By this time, the Russian leadership realised the need to strengthen the eastern vector of its foreign policy, including restoring relations with Mongolia. It is important to note that one of Putin's earliest foreign trips as President was to visit Mongolia on 13 November 2000. The visit was short but intense where Putin met with the President of Mongolia, Natsagiin Bagabandi, with the Chairman of the State Great Khural Lhamsurengiin and Prime Minister Nambaryn Enkhbayar.[77] At the end of the visit, the Russian President laid a wreath at the monument to Soviet soldiers on Mount Zaisan, erected in honour of the victory of Mongolian and Soviet troops at Khalkhin Gol in 1939.[78]

The main result of this visit was the adoption of the "Ulan Bator Declaration". In this document, Mongolia and Russia stated the commonality or similarity of approaches to critical problems of the time; both sides spoke in favour of building up interaction in world affairs, for closer cooperation in the UN and other international organisations, in particular, for strengthening the regime of non-proliferation of weapons of mass destruction, the fight against international terrorism, increasing the effectiveness and efficiency of the UN, carrying out a rational reform of the UN Security Council.[79] The declaration identified a wide range of issues on which both sides agreed to mutually beneficial cooperation, including trade and economic, military, cultural and humanitarian.

Thus, the Ulan Bator Declaration became the second important general political document concluded between Russia and Mongolia after the Treaty on Friendly

Relations and Cooperation. The declaration secured the transition to a qualitatively new level of contacts between Russia and Mongolia and also contributed to the successful solution of several thorny issues, primarily the sizeable unpaid debt of Soviet loans granted to Mongolia. There were different opinions in Mongolia about the origin of Mongolia's enormous debt to the USSR, but it was clear that such a problem was an obstacle to the further development of relations.[80]

Mongolia's debt to Russia was very worrying in the years after independence, especially in the early 2000s. One view concerned that the solution to this issue would be for Russia to meet its southern neighbour halfway since the amount of debt was more than twice the country's GDP at that time, and Mongolia was unable to pay it off. The matter was finally resolved in 2004 whereby Mongolia made a payment of less than $300 million, in return for which a massive Soviet debt of $ 11.4 billion was written off.[81] This was almost all of the debt accounting for 97% of the total. Six years later, "as a result of bilateral negotiations held in July 2010, the sides managed to reach an agreement, under which Mongolia undertook to repay financial obligations worth 163.7 million convertible rubles and 10.5 million clearing US dollars with a lump sum payment of $3.8 million" to settle the entire debt.[82]

The adoption of the Ulan Bator Declaration contributed to the further development of the regulatory framework of relations. Thus, several intergovernmental agreements were concluded: on cooperation on the peaceful use of atomic energy, on the principles of cooperation between the executive authorities of the constituent entities of the Russian Federation and local administrations of Mongolia, on cooperation in tourism, on the provision of military-technical assistance to Mongolia free of charge, on mutual recognition of educational documents, academic degrees and academic titles. [83] After resolving the debt problem, Russian positions in Mongolia began to gradually strengthen, with the practice of exchanging high-level visits resuming.[84] A notable visit took place in April 2000, when the Secretary of the National Security Council of Mongolia Ravdangiin Bold paid a visit to Moscow; in September of the same year, his Russian colleague Ivanov returned the visit.[85]

Table: 2 Official Visits by Mongolian Presidents to Russia

President	Years
Punsalmaagiin Ochirbat	1998
Natsagiin Bagabandi	1999, 2005
Nambaryn Enkhbayar	2006, 2008
Tsakhiagiin Elbegdorj	2010, 2011, 2015
Khaltmaagiin Battulga	2017, 2018, 2019

Source: Open Sources

Parliamentary ties also developed alongside the improvement of military cooperation between the two countries.[86] It should be noted that given the long-term presence of Soviet troops on the territory of Mongolia, which complicated Mongolia's relations with China, modern Mongolia approached the issue of military cooperation with other states very carefully. Pursuing a peaceful foreign policy, Mongolia, nevertheless, in the 1992 Constitution enshrined the following principle in Article 4: "Stationing of foreign troops in the territory of Mongolia or admitting over the state border to traverse shall be prohibited without enactment of a law."[87] This did not exclude the possibility of developing military ties with other states to ensure Mongolia's security, which included Russia.[88] As seen in Table: 2, the practice of high-level meetings continued in subsequent years.[89]

A significant milestone in developing strategic relations between the two countries was the state visit of the President of Mongolia Nambaryn Enkhbayar to Moscow in December 2006.[90] During this visit, several intergovernmental agreements were concluded to diversify relations in various fields and improve the legal framework. However, the main result of the visit was the signing of the "Moscow Declaration", in which all the previously reached agreements were confirmed.[91] The document stated the desire of the parties to seek to improve the efficiency and scale of interaction in the spirit of a strategic partner state, which presupposed taking relations to an even higher and qualitatively new level. It is essential to state here that both sides had declared their desire to move forward along the path of strategic partnership.

The strategic nature of relations was consolidated in August 2009 during the visit of Russian President Medvedev to Ulaanbaatar by signing the "Declaration on the Development of Strategic Partnership" between Russia and Mongolia.[92] The parties expressed their readiness for closer cooperation in such strategically important areas as transport infrastructure, cooperation in all types of energy resources, and cooperation in agriculture and cross-border trade. One must underline the fact that all three of the above-mentioned declarations define the strategy of the Mongolian-Russian partnership, namely: the intensification of cooperation in all areas, the all-round strengthening of political ties, an increase in trade turnover, the growth of investment projects, the development and implementation of long-term programs in the economy, science and culture, the expansion of cross-border cooperation and regional integration. One should also note that these declarations, along with the 1993 Treaty and more than 130 intergovernmental and interdepartmental agreements concluded after 1993, have become a stable legal basis for the development of bilateral relations.

After the Medvedev visit in 2009, President Putin, on 3 September 2014, contributed to the deepening and intensification of the strategic partnership between the Russian Federation and Mongolia.[93] His visit was timed to coincide with the 75th anniversary of the victory of the Soviet and Mongolian troops on the Khalkhin-Gol River over the Japanese. Honouring the memory of Soviet and Mongolian soldiers, Putin reiterated the shared historical memory, heroic comradeship of the past, forming a sound basis for building modern Russian-Mongolian relations in the spirit of mutual respect, trust and friendship.

As a result of Putin's negotiations with the President of Mongolia, Tsakhiagiin Elbegdorj, 15 intergovernmental, interdepartmental and sectoral agreements were signed. Among them: Agreement between the Ministry of Roads and Transport of Mongolia and JSC Russian Railways on strategic partnership for the modernisation and development of the Ulaanbaatar Railway (UBZhD), Memorandum between the Ministry of Economic Development, the Russian Federation and the Ministry of Economic Development of Mongolia on cooperation in the development of Russian-Mongolian economic relations, the Memorandum of Understanding between Aeroflot and MIAT - Mongolian Airlines, providing for the expansion of cooperation in the field of civil aviation and the air route network.[94]

Cross-Border Cooperation: Buryatia

When focusing closely on the history of Russian-Mongolian cross-border cooperation, both entities have centuries of experience in political, trade and economic and cultural interaction. Outer Mongolia or Northern Mongolia (Khalkha) since 1691 became part of the Chinese Qing Empire.[95] In establishing Russian-Mongolian ties, a unique role was played by Eastern Siberia. The development of Russian-Mongolian relations was based on treaties between the Russian Empire and China – Nerchinsky (1689), Burinsky and Kyakhtinsky (1727).[96] By including Mongolia in the Qing Empire, the Manchus created a particular system of government on its territory. Mongolia was inundated with Chinese merchants who controlled the market. Chinese merchants were represented here by large firms that, for their part, exerted intense pressure on the Chinese government, demanding the prevention of Russian merchants from entering Mongolia. An important role in bilateral relations was also played by Russian merchants interested in the Mongolian market.[97]

The main competition for Russian merchants in the Mongolian market was Chinese traders who imported goods from Western countries and acted as intermediaries of foreign firms. Russian-Chinese trade went mainly through the "eastern gate" to Asia - the trading settlement of Kyakhta.[98] This main trading centre in Eastern Siberia accounted for a majority of commodity turnover of Russia with Asian countries. Before the opening of seaports and the construction of the Trans-Siberian Railway, the Kyakhta road was the main transit point of the Great Tea Route.[99] On the other side of the border, three kilometres from Kyakhta, in the city of Maimacheng, the bulk of Russian-Chinese and Russian-Mongolian trade took place.[100] In 1921, after the city's capture by units of the Mongolian People's Army under the command of Sukhbaataar, its name was changed to Altanbulag and became one of the centres of revolutionary forces.[101]

After Mongolia achieved independence, the Russian-Mongolian trade was regulated by the Russian-Mongolian agreement of 1912.[102] The Mongolian government provided Russian merchants with the rights and advantages listed in the attached trade protocol and pledged not to provide other foreign subjects with greater rights than those enjoyed by the Russians. In other words, the Russian-Mongolian agreement of 1912 and the protocol favoured Russian trade as much as possible, which led to its noticeable growth. It should be recalled, however, that Russian-Mongolian relations passed through difficult stages of formation and development. In the pre-revolutionary period, Russia provided assistance to promote Mongolia in maintaining its independence, and in Soviet times acted in the role of patron, provided military, material and financial assistance to the fraternal Republic. During the Soviet era, foreign trade and economic relations were thoroughly planned from the union centre.

In the early 1990s in foreign policy, there was a certain underestimation of its eastern direction and weakening attention to relationships with traditional friendly partners. In the post-socialist period, the reorientation towards cross-border cooperation was caused by the curtailment of interstate labour and a natural reaction to the economic crisis. Respectively the primary role in the preservation and development of cooperation had to be played by the local regions of Siberia.[103]

Only at the end of the last decade of the twentieth century did the ties between Russia and Mongolia start to revive, building on the principles of equality. The bulk of trade between Russia and Mongolia fell on the Irkutsk region, the Trans-Baikal Territory, the Republic of Buryatia, Altai and Tuva.[104] Representative offices worked in close cooperation with trade and industry chambers and embassies of Russia and Mongolia. Particular attention was paid to the representatives of border regions of Russia concerning the problems of strengthening the material base and increasing transport capacity; as there were 29 checkpoints on the Russian-Mongolian border, formerly only 5 were the main ones: in Kyakhta, Shara Sume, Tsagaan Tolgoit, Khandagaite and Tashanthe.[105] Thus, modern Russian-Mongolian relations are developing progressively and trending towards a qualitatively new level of an all-encompassing strategic partnership.

At the same time, it should be noted that significant obstacles to the development of Russian-Mongolian are a phenomenal imbalance in mutual trade, high customs duties and fees, transportation costs, various sanitary and veterinary restrictions for some Mongolian export goods.[106] Under these conditions, Ulaanbaatar's view is for Russia to go beyond the declarative nature of bilateral relations and take tangible steps and intensify efforts in the political, trade, economic, educational and cultural and humanitarian spheres.

Buryatia has long-standing historical ties with Mongolia, which have been developed to deepen trade and economic cooperation between the Republic of Buryatia and Mongolia since the 2000s.[107] Cooperation between the Republic of Buryatia and Mongolia is carried out within the framework of bilateral agreements between the two countries.

Table: 3 Mongolian Exports to Russia (2019)

	Value $ Millions
Salt, sulphur, earth, stone, plaster, lime and cement	49.43
Mineral fuels, oils, distillation products	10.39
Articles of apparel, knit or crocheted	2.98
Machinery, nuclear reactors, boilers	1.07
Wool, animal hair, horsehair yarn and fabric	0.784

Source: Trading Economics. (n.d.). Mongolia exports to Russia. Retrieved July 31, 2021, from https://tradingeconomics.com/mongolia/exports/russia

Table: 4 Mongolian Imports from Russia (2019)

	Value $ Millions
Mineral fuels, oils, distillation products	1,150
Iron and steel	74.02
Aircraft, spacecraft	50.0
Machinery, nuclear reactors, boilers	49.37
Fertilisers	38.07

Source: Trading Economics. (n.d.). Mongolia imports from Russia. Retrieved July 31, 2021, from https://tradingeconomics.com/mongolia/imports/russia

Cross-border cooperation is carried out in traditional spheres: foreign trade, investment cooperation, joint activities in agriculture, environmental protection, tourism and sports, education and science, culture and healthcare. The main imports from Mongolia are meat and food offal.[108] The structure of Buryat exports to Mongolia fits in with the general Russian exports identified in Table: 3, represented by food products, engineering products: aircraft, equipment and electrical machines.[109] Foreign trade cooperation with Mongolia is diverse as Table: 4 demonstrates a wide range of trade and economic relations between the two countries. The Republic of Buryatia and Mongolia gives much importance to develop trade and economic cooperation to interstate meetings.[110] These involve not only non-governmental structures but also business barters and public figures.[111]

However, trade and economic relations between the Republic of Buryatia and Mongolia are varied, including a wide range of supplies and products. The export deliveries of the Republic of Buryatia to Mongolia make up the supply of fish, bread products and flour confectionery products and breeding cattle. A priority area in developing cooperation to promote from Mongolia to the Republic of Belarus remains beef and horse meat supply. Such endeavours give credence to the assertion that foreign trade cooperation with Mongolia is actively developing, especially in recent years.[112] A limiting factor in the supply of raw meat from Mongolia today is also the high cost of Mongolian meat.[113]

The main problem in cross-border cooperation between the Republic of Buryatia and Mongolia today is health fears. Mongolia is considered a risk factor regarding ofru, brucellosis, anthrax, goat pox, glanders, equine infectious anaemia, cattle tuberculosis.[114] Existing restrictions on imports from Mongolia cattle, horses, and small ruminants due to high epizootic risks cannot be cancelled until the epizootic situation stabilises. The main focus in the development of trade and economic cooperation is to solve issues of promoting Buryat manufacturers' products to the Mongolian market.

Since the late 1990s, bilateral relations have been based on new principles of equal partnership. Currently, bilateral relations have been brought to a new level of comprehensive strategic partnership. In this regard, the border areas are to carry out a special mission to establish an effective interstate natural interaction and cooperation. As a border region, Buryatia has a long history based on economic, political, cultural, humanitarian ties. Investigating the trade and economic cooperation between Mongolia and the region demonstrates a high potential for trade and economic development and investment cooperation. Particular attention for both sides in terms of opportunities for investment and cooperation concerns the creation at the Russian-Mongolian border, the free trade zone Altanbulag.[115] Built on the legendary Maimacheng of the 18th century, Altanbulag in the future has the potential to become a pole of growth of the national economy and the border regions of Siberia. Favourable geographical position at the intersection of transit routes from Asia to Europe and the development of Russian-Mongolian trade relations has lent credibility to consider it a free trade zone prototype. One of the promising areas for development is tourism, part of a cooperation between Mongolia and Buryatia; another is to further develop cooperation in the educational sphere.[116]

However, there are obstacles to practical cross-border cooperation. The cooperation of Buryatia and Mongolia is limited by the narrowness of the range of export goods, high customs tariffs for traditional export goods, high phytosanitary and veterinary requirements for the export of Mongolian meat production, and the competition of Buryatia with other Russian regions.[117] In order to be successful, it is necessary to save the accumulated potential and move forward, be actively involved in the process interaction at the interstate and regional levels, and actively develop horizontal links between aimags - districts, cities, cultures and cultures educational institutions.

Conclusion

Concerning bilateral relations, Russian Foreign Minister Lavrov, at a joint news conference following talks with his Mongolian counterpart Battsetseg in Moscow on 1 June 2021, stated the "mutual resolve to continue strengthening our ties in the spirit of the Treaty on Friendly Relations and Comprehensive Strategic Partnership, which our presidents signed in Ulaanbaatar in September 2019."[118] Whilst encouraging the activities of the Russian-Mongolian Intergovernmental Commission on Trade and Economic, Scientific and Technical Cooperation, previous successful cooperation in the technical and exploration fields were also highlighted when Lavrov noted the "40th anniversary of the joint Soviet-Mongolian space mission. Immediately after this news conference, we will hold a ceremony to present the Order of Alexander Nevsky to pilot-cosmonaut Jugderdemidiin Gurragchaa, President of the Mongolia-Russia Friendship Society, Hero of the Soviet Union and Hero of Mongolia." Issues relating to security cooperation affecting the SCO, OSCE and other Asian forums were also discussed with economic matters being emphasized, Lavrov declaring that "Talks are underway between Mongolia and the Eurasian Economic Commission on the possible signing of a free trade zone agreement, which will help boost our economic ties."[119]

The very next month Lavrov in his address concerning Russia's International Activities for Russian Regions' Development in Vladivostok on 8 July 2021, made public that the "EAEU and China are now discussing projects that can form the backbone of the Greater Eurasian Partnership. I'm talking about economic corridors that will help reinvigorate the region and lift up entire industries. We will see this fairly soon as the Russia - Mongolia - China corridor becomes a reality."[120] Referring to the Far Eastern region, Lavrov reiterated that "One of the main priorities for our diplomacy is using the large-scale potential of the Asia-Pacific Region to boost the comprehensive development of the Russian Far East and improve the well-being of local residents. In accordance with the presidential instructions, the Government of the Russian Federation is taking systemic measures to enhance the role of the Far Eastern Federal District as an economic hub for interaction with the countries in the region and is doing its best to ensure the largest possible practical effect from international cooperation. We have been pursuing this line at APEC, which held its summit meeting at FEFU in 2012. The spread of the coronavirus has certainly taken its toll on the efforts to implement investment opportunities in the Russian Far East. However, the progress made in recent years, including as regards the "priority development areas," the open port of Vladivostok and special economic zones, allows us to move forward with confidence. The Asia-Pacific countries are participating in energy and transport programmes, and are also investing in healthcare, food and chemical industry projects. The volume of transit cargo hauled via the Trans-Siberian Railway and the Northern Sea Route is growing. Scientific and academic ties are expanding, and the University is well aware of all this. Almost two-thirds of the foreign direct investment attracted to the Russian Far East comes from China. This includes over 50 projects in a whole variety of fields. We are trying to maximise the use of these investments for breakthrough projects in order to increase our competitiveness."[121]

The year 2021 marks the centenary of the establishment of diplomatic relations between Russia and Mongolia. The two statements made by Lavrov demonstrate that in this anniversary year, Moscow foresees closer collaboration and cooperation. Economically speaking, Russia is no longer the dominant partner Mongolia cherished during the Cold War. Nor is it the military superpower vying for global preeminence. Its cultural impact is also on the wane in Mongolian society, which has become more globalised and been introduced to regions and languages beyond the Russo-sphere.

Nevertheless, from the moment of the proclamation of independence from the Qing Empire in 1911 until the end of the 1980s, the history of Mongolia was closely connected with the Czarist Empire and its successor, the USSR. Russia supported the Mongols in their desire to secede from the Qing Empire and played the central role in the proclamation of independence, providing them with significant assistance in building statehood.

In a short period, Mongolia emerged from the backward outskirts of the Qing Empire with a population almost on the verge of extinction as an aspiring modern, developed state.[122] The USSR became Mongolia's loyal ally, sponsor, and guarantor of both territorial integrity and sovereignty. In turn, it must be stated that Mongolia also played an important role in Russian history, having influenced the unification process of the Russian lands during the Middle Ages. The Russians adopted from the Mongol-Tatars the specificities of statehood, military and financial systems, and the methods of diplomacy.[123]

In the 20th century, Mongolia's role in foreign policy was significant for the USSR. Mongolia's aid to the Soviet people during the Second World War too was extremely welcome. It served as a buffer between the USSR and the People's Republic of China during their intricate relations, resulting in the Sino-Soviet split. Thus, Mongolia was one of the first foreign countries to express its readiness to help the Soviet Union immediately after the start of World War II; and in certain respects, its various measures of assistance was comparable in principle to that of Lend-Lease.[124]

Thus, analysing bilateral relations between Mongolia and Russia, one can conclude that both parties have undertaken much work over the last thirty years. Mongolia and Russia have gone from restoring relations to establishing a strategic partnership. A solid regulatory framework has been created for the development of relations in multiple directions, the practice of regular meetings at a high level has developed, and trade and economic ties continue to progress. Nevertheless, it should be recalled that Russia's influence in Mongolia is incomparable to the Soviet period. Mongolia successfully developed relations with countries such as the United States, Canada, Turkey, and Australia, geographically located at considerable distances from Northeast Asia. Quite naturally, this strategy of Mongolia is conditioned by the concept of a "third neighbour", adopted in opposition to Russia and China.[125]

President Putin proposed developing a road map for further cooperation to create new industries, stimulate trade and mutual investment, and expand humanitarian contacts.[126] Throughout the 2010s, Russia has clearly indicated its desire to strengthen its political, economic and cultural influence in Mongolia. One may term this strategy a possible return to Mongolia. Nevertheless, the emerging situation in the APR, namely the growing military power of the PRC, a possible reduction in the US presence in the APR, as was repeatedly stated by the Trump Administration, may lead to a re-equilibration of the balance of power in this region, which may not meet the interests of either Mongolia or Russia. Consequently, Mongolia and Russia may need to consider strengthening their cooperation to maintain the balance of power in the region.

References

1 Haining, T. N. (1991). Elevated-by-all!. Asian Affairs, 22(2), 167-175.

2 Mandal, R. (2012). Ch'ing Policies towards Mongols and its Impact on Mongolian National Movement. Academic Discourse, 1(2), 17-25.

3 Dennis, A. L. (1923). Russian Policy in the Far East. The North American Review, 217(808), 303-312.

4 ELLEMAN, B. A. (1994). SOVIET POLICY ON OUTER MONGOLIA AND

THE CHINESE COMMUNIST PARTY. Journal of Asian History, 28(2), 108-123.

5 Kuznetsov, I. I. (1999). The Soviet military advisors in Mongolia 1921–39. The Journal of Slavic Military Studies, 12(4), 118-137.

6 Halperin, C. J. (1982). Tsarev ulus: Russia in the Golden Horde. Cahiers du Monde russe et soviétique, 257-263., Halperin, C. J. (1982). " Know Thy Enemy": Medieval Russian Familiarity with the Mongols of the Golden Horde. Jahrbücher für Geschichte Osteuropas, (H. 2), 161-175.

7 Kamalov, A. (2018). Russkiye konsulstva v Sintsiane (konets XIX–nachalo XX vv.)[Russian consulates in Xinjiang (late XIX–early XX centuries)], 180-183.

8 Qurbonovich, O. A. (2019). International Relations in the Far East and Russia in the Late 19th and Early 20th Centuries. Indonesian Journal of Innovation Studies, 5.

9 Kurguzov, P.V. (2019). TO THE HISTORY OF THE FORMATION OF THE URGA ORDER OF ATAMAN SEMENOV ON THE TERRITORY OF OUTER MONGOLIA IN 1918 IN THE MODERN WORLD, 288.

10 Sizova, A. (2016). The Political Role of the Russian Consulates in Mongolia in the Mongolian National Liberation Movement in the Early 20th Century. Higher School of Economics Research Paper No. WP BRP, 119.

11 Garbutt, P. E. (1954). The Trans-Siberian Railway. The Journal of Transport History, (4), 238-249.

12 Wiren, A. R. (1942). The Lesson of Port Arthur. Russian Review, 1(2), 40-43.

13 Tolstoguzov, S. (2016, July). Russian–Japanese relations after the Russo-Japanese war in the context of world politics. In Japan forum (Vol. 28, No. 3, pp. 282-298). Routledge.

14 Ewing, T. E. (1980). Ch'ing Policies in Outer Mongolia 1900–1911. Modern Asian Studies, 14(1), 145-157.

15 Lee, C. (2014). From Kitchen to Vladivostok: Russian Merchants and the Tea Trade. Region: Regional Studies of Russia, Eastern Europe, and Central Asia, 3(2), 195-218.

16 Popova, I. F. (2008). Russian Explorations in Central Asia at the Turn of the 20th Century. St. Petersburg. (Russian Explorations in Central Asia at the Turn of the 20th Century, St Petersburg, 2008. http://www. iop. or. jp/Documents/1727/12_% 5B104-126% 5DI. F. Popova. pdf 104-126).

17 Kozloff, P. K. (1909). The Mongolia-Sze-Chuan expedition of the Imperial Rus-

sian Geographical Society. The Geographical Journal, 34(4), 384-408.

18 Dear, D. (2014). Holy Rollers: Monasteries, Lamas, and the Unseen Transport of Chinese–Russian Trade, 1850–1911. International Review of Social History, 59(S22), 69-88.

19 Bridges, F. (1945). Peace in Mongolia. Current History, 9(50), 311-316.

20 Basu, S. A. (1978). Mongolia between Russia and China.

21 Hyer, E. A. (2005). Haunted by History: China and Its Northwestern Neighbors. Historia Actual Online, (7), 83-92.

22 Boardman, E. P. (1951). Gerard M. Fritters, Outer Mongolia and its international position, tr. by John De Francis Edited by Meribeth E. Cameron and Osamu Shimizu (Book Review). Journal of Asian Studies, 10(2), 199.

23 Wiens, H. J. (1950). Outer Mongolia and Its International Position.

24 Kozloff, P. K. (1910). The Mongolia-Sze-Chuan expedition of the Imperial Russian Geographical Society. The Geographical Journal, 36(3), 288-310.

25 Pestushko, Y. S., & Shulatov, Y. A. (2019). Russo-Japanese Relations from 1905 to 1916: from Enemies to Allies. In A History of Russo-Japanese Relations (pp. 101-118). Brill.

26 Masahiro, H. O. S. H. I. N. O. (2000). A Historical Examination of the Founding of Inner Mongolia Autonomous Region. CHINA'S BORDERLAND HISTORY AND GEOGRAPHY STUDIES., Clauson, G. (1956). The case against the Altaic theory. Central Asiatic Journal, 181-187.

27 Síma, J. (1974). On the Character of the So-Called Pan-Mongol Movement After 1911. Archív Orientální, 42, 97-119., Bayarkhuu, D. (2001). Mongolia and its Third Neighbours. Himalayan and Central Asian Studies, 5(1), 80.,

28 Williams, E. T. (1916). The Relations Between China, Russia and Mongolia. American Journal of International Law, 10(4), 798-808.,

29 Urangua, J., Kuzmin, Yu.V., Vasilenko, V.A., & Karasev, S.V. (2020). History of world and Russian Mongol studies: national schools, problems, personalities. Bulletin of the laboratory of ancient technologies, 16 (3), 188-196.

30 Guzalovich, K. A. The "Mongolian question" to Russian foreign policy. International Journal on Integrated Education, 2(6), 67-72.

31 Maghame, B. (1973). CHINESE POLICY TOWARD TIBET AND MONGOLIA. California State University, Fullerton.,

32 Jianyong, F. (2013). The "political game" and "state-building": outer Mongolia during the 1911 Revolution. In China (pp. 275-293). Routledge.

33 Chih-Yi, M. C. (1950). Bibliography of books and articles on Mongolia.,

34 Spring, D. W. (1979). Russian imperialism in Asia in 1914. Cahiers du monde russe et soviétique, 305-322.

35 Saveliev, I. R., & Pestushko, Y. S. (2001). Dangerous Rapprochement: Russia and Japan in the First World War, 1914–1916. Acta Slavica Iaponica, 18, 19-41.

36 Síma, J. (1974). On the Character of the So-Called Pan-Mongol Movement After 1911. Archív Orientální, 42, 97-119.

37 Urbansky, S. (2020). 3. Revolutions without Borders. In Beyond the Steppe Frontier (pp. 89-122). Princeton University Press.

38 Lepekhov, S. Y. (2013). The Religious Policy of the Russian Government towards Buddhism at the End of the 19th and Beginning of the 20th Centuries. International Journal of Buddhist Thought and Culture, 20, 145-161.

39 Yigit, S. (2020). Tuva, April 1914: Incorporation as a Russian Protectorate. International Relations and Diplomacy, 8(07), 281-289.

40 Hyer, E. A. (2005). Haunted by History: China and Its Northwestern Neighbors. Historia Actual Online, (7), 83-92.

41 Valliant, R. B. (1977). Inner Mongolia, 1912: the Failure of Independence. Mongolian Studies, 56-92.

42 Chen, T. H. E. (1955). RUSSIA'S FAR EASTERN POLICY. Current history, 28(162), 95-102., Strausz-Hupé, R. (1950). MANCHURIA AND MONGOLIA: RED AND WHITE IMPERIALISM. Current History, 19(108), 73-77.

43 Boikova, E. (2002). Russians in Mongolia in the Late 19 th-Early 20 the Centuries. Mongolian Studies, 13-20.

44 Endicott, E. (2012). Agriculture, Mining, Tourism: Competing Interests in Land Use. In A History of Land Use in Mongolia (pp. 129-157). Palgrave Macmillan, New York.

45 Haining, T. N. (1996). The Yak, the Bear and the Dragon: Uneasy Bedfellows. A Cautionary Tale of Russian and Chinese Influences on Mongolian History. Journal of the Royal Asiatic Society, 6(1), 69-79.

46 Endicott, E. (2005). The Mongols and China: cultural contacts and the changing nature of pastoral nomadism (twelfth to early twentieth centuries). BRILL'S INNER ASIAN LIBRARY, 461.

47 Boikova, E. (2002). Russians in Mongolia in the Late 19 th-Early 20 the Centuries. Mongolian Studies, 13-20.

48 Ewing, T. E. (1981). The Forgotten Frontier: South Siberia (Tuva) in Chinese

and Russian History, 1600-1920. Central Asiatic Journal, 25(3/4), 174-212.

49 Ewing, T. E. (1978). The Origin of the Mongolian People's Revolutionary Party: 1920. Mongolian Studies, 79-105., Polyanskaya, O. (2014). Professor Władysław L. Kotwicz and the Russian Committee of Central and East Asia Research. Rocznik Orientalistyczny, (1)., Miller, R. J. (1952). A selective survey of literature on Mongolia. American Political Science Review, 46(3), 849-866., Ivanov, A. A., Kuras, L. V., Kuras, S. L., & Kuras, T. L. (2020, January). From the History of the Gendarme Police Service Organization on the Trans-Baikal Railway (1899–1917). In International Session on Factors of Regional Extensive Development (FRED 2019) (pp. 520-525). Atlantis Press.,

50 Rupen, R. A. (1958). Mongolian nationalism. Journal of the Royal Central Asian Society, 45(2), 157-178.

51 Nekrylov, S. A. (2014). Russian and international scientific and educational contacts among professors and teachers as a form of organisation for scientific work and the improvement of teaching and research skills (based on the example of Tomsk State University). History of Medicine, 3, 78-84.

52 Sizova, A. (2016). The Political Role of the Russian Consulates in Mongolia in the Mongolian National Liberation Movement in the Early 20th Century. Higher School of Economics Research Paper No. WP BRP, 119.

53 Peshkov, I. (2017). In the shadow of 'frontier disloyalty' at Russia–China–Mongolia border zones. History and Anthropology, 28(4), 429-444.

54 Mansvetov, F. S. (1945). Russia and China in Outer Mongolia. Foreign affairs, 24(1), 143-152.

55 Sarlagtay, M. O. (2004). Mongolia: Managing transition from nomadic to settled culture. The Asia-Pacific: A region in transition, 323-334.

56 Mongolia's Constitution of 1992 with Amendments through 2001. (n.d.). Retrieved July 31, 2021, from https://www.constituteproject.org/constitution/Mongolia_2001.pdf.

57 Rodionov, V., Aktamov, I., Badaraev, D., Badmatsyrenov, T., Kombaev, A., & Dorzhieva, I. (2016). Foreign powers competition in the mining sector of Mongolia. In SHS Web of Conferences (Vol. 28, p. 01137). EDP Sciences.

58 Severinghaus, S. R. (2001). Mongolia in 2000 the pendulum swings again. Asian Survey, 41(1), 61-70.

59 Rozman, G. (2018). The Russian Pivot to Asia. In International Relations and Asia's Northern Tier (pp. 13-26). Palgrave, Singapore.

60 Rangsimaporn, P. (2009). Russian perceptions and policies in a multipolar East

Asia under Yeltsin and Putin. International Relations of the Asia-Pacific, 9(2), 207-244.

61 Pieper, M. (2020). The new silk road heads north: implications of the China-Mongolia-Russia economic corridor for Mongolian agency within Eurasian power shifts. Eurasian Geography and Economics, 1-24.

62 World Bank. (n.d.). GDP growth (annual %) - Mongolia. Retrieved July 31, 2021, from https://data.worldbank.org/indicator/NY.GDP.MKTP.KD.ZG?end=2020&locations=MN&start=1982&view=chart

63 Rodionov, V., Badmatsyrenov, T., Aktamov, I., & Badaraev, D. (2017, June). Economic security of Mongolia in context of Northeast Asia prospects. In International Conference on Trends of Technologies and Innovations in Economic and Social Studies 2017 (pp. 557-562). Atlantis Press.

64 World Bank. (n.d.). Mongolia trade. Retrieved July 31, 2021, from https://wits.worldbank.org/countrysnapshot/en/MNG

65 Ganhuyag, E. (2017). RUSSIA-MONGOLIA FROM THE 1990S TO 2016: ON THE WAY OF STRATEGIC PARTNERSHIP. RUDN Journal of Russian History, 16(3), 462-476.

66 Batbayar, T. (2003). Mongolian-Russian relations in the past decade. Asian Survey, 43(6), 951-970.

67 Sneath, D. (2020, October 23). Russia's borders: Mongolia looks to its old Big brother to counterbalance China. Retrieved July 31, 2021, from https://theconversation.com/russias-borders-mongolia-looks-to-its-old-big-brother-to-counterbalance-china-36721

68 Dzhagaeva, O. A. (2019). SOME PROBLEMS OF SOVIET-MONGOL COOPERATION. Caspian region: politics, economics, culture, (2 (59)), 42-47.

69 Ganhuyag, E. (2017). RUSSIA-MONGOLIA FROM THE 1990S TO 2016: ON THE WAY OF STRATEGIC PARTNERSHIP. RUDN Journal of Russian History, 16(3), 462-476.

70 Reinert, E. S. (2004). Globalisation in the Periphery as a Morgenthau Plan: The Underdevelopment of Mongolia in the 1990s. Globalisation, economic development and inequality: An alternative perspective, 157-214.

71 Batbayar, T. (1994). Mongolia in 1993: a fragile democracy. Asian Survey, 34(1), 41-45.

72 Ivanov, I., & Erdenechuluun, L. (2005). Joint Russian-Mongolian Statement. Mongolian Journal of International Affairs, (12), 107-111.

73 Radchenko, S. (2012). Soviet Withdrawal from Mongolia, 1986–1992: A Reas-

sessment. The Journal of Slavic Military Studies, 25(2), 183-203.

74 Ganhuyag, E. (2017). RUSSIA-MONGOLIA FROM THE 1990S TO 2016: ON THE WAY OF STRATEGIC PARTNERSHIP. RUDN Journal of Russian History, 16(3), 462-476.

75 Batbayar, T. (2003). Mongolian-Russian relations in the past decade. Asian Survey, 43(6), 951-970.

76 McFaul, M. (2000). Putin in power. Current History, 99(639), 307-314.

77 Severinghaus, S. R. (2001). Mongolia in 2000 the pendulum swings again. Asian Survey, 41(1), 61-70.

78 Trifonova, A.A. (2020). To be remembered. Diplomatic Service, (2), 79-83.

79 Krishna, V. (2018). Expanding Vistas of Mongolia-Russia Strategic Partnership since 2000 Ulaanbaatar Declaration. Mongolian Journal of International Affairs, 20, 101-114.

80 Sumiyabazar, C. (2004). Mongolia: Forgiven—The Mongolian government hails record Russian debt write-off. But was there really anything to be forgiven?. Week in review, 13-19.

81 Panda, A. (2016, February 03). Why did Russia just write off 97% of Mongolian debt? Retrieved July 31, 2021, from https://thediplomat.com/2016/02/why-did-russia-just-write-off-97-of-mongolian-debt/

82 ibid.

83 Sagaev, N. T., & Dugarov, V. D. (2012). COOPERATION BETWEEN THE USSR AND MPR IN EDUCATION AND SCIENCE IN THE XX CENTURY IN THE NATIONAL HISTORIOGRAPHY. Bulletin of the East Siberian State University of Technology/Vestnik VSGTU, 38(3).

84 In January 2001, in Davos, the Prime Minister of Mongolia Enkhbayar met with the Deputy Prime Minister of Russia, Kudrin; in February 2001, Deputy Chairman of the State Great Khural of Mongolia Zhamsran Byam-badorj and Minister of Justice and Internal Affairs Tsendiin Nyamdorj visited Moscow. Also, in February 2001, the 2nd meeting of the working group on the liberalisation of mutual trade was held in Ulaanbaatar. Moreover, cooperation began to be developed through the security councils of the two countries.

85 Batbayar, T. (2003). Foreign policy and domestic reform in Mongolia. Central Asian Survey, 22(1), 45-59.

86 In February 2002, a delegation headed by the Chairman of the State Great Khural of Mongolia Sangzhbegziin Tumur-Ochir paid an official visit to Moscow. During the meetings, Tumur-Ochir spoke about expanding contacts with Rus-

sia in culture, education and science. He emphasised that in Mongolia, after a sure decline, there was a growing interest in education in Russia, in the Russian language. In response, a delegation of the State Duma of the Russian Federation was planned to visit Mongolia. Subsequently, meetings of parliamentarians of both countries took place.

87 Bedeski, R. E. (2006). Mongolia as a Modern Sovereign Nation-State. Mongolian Journal of International Affairs, (13), 77-87.

88 During this visit in October 2000, A.V. Kvashnin - Chief of the General Staff of the Russian Armed Forces, the Action Plan for military cooperation between the armed forces of the Russian Federation and Mongolia for 2001 and the Memorandum of Intent between the RF Ministry of Defense and the Mongolian Defense Ministry on the development of cooperation in the military field were signed. In March 2001, a Russian military delegation headed by Deputy Chief of the General Staff of the Russian Armed Forces A.S. Skvortsov took part in events dedicated to the 80th anniversary of the Armed Forces of Mongolia. On April 15-22, 2001, the Mongolian Defense Minister ZhYgderdemidiin Gurragchi, the first Mongolian cosmonaut, paid an official visit to Moscow.

89 In March 2006, Russian Foreign Minister Sergei Lavrov paid a working visit to Ulan Bator, and in July 2006, Russian Prime Minister Mikhail Fradkov paid an official visit to Mongolia. During his talks with his Mongolian counterpart, Mieegombyn Enkhbold, serious attention was paid to trade and economic cooperation, including Russia's participation in large investment projects.

90 Graivoronsky, V. V. (2014). Russia's Role in the Exploration and Development of Natural Resources in Contemporary Mongolia. Inner Asia, 16(2), 315-335.

91 Shen, Q. (2016). Analysis of Sino-Russia-Magnolia Trade Cooperation Potential: Based on the Perspective of Trade Gravity Model. J]. Advances in Social Science, Education and Humanities Research, 91.

92 Bulag, U. E. (2010). Mongolia in 2009: from landlocked to land-linked cosmopolitan. Asian Survey, 50(1), 97-103.

93 Fan, L. (2017). Construction of Russia's "Eurasian Union" and "Economic Corridor among China, Mongolia, and Russia". In China's Belt and Road Initiatives and Its Neighboring Diplomacy (pp. 83-107).

94 Fan, L. (2017). Construction of Russia's "Eurasian Union" and "Economic Corridor among China, Mongolia, and Russia". In China's Belt and Road Initiatives and Its Neighboring Diplomacy (pp. 83-107., Jargalsaikhan, M. (2018). Mongolia's Dilemma: A Politically Linked, Economically Isolated Small Power. In International Relations and Asia's Northern Tier (pp. 157-173). Palgrave,

Singapore.

95 Ginsburg, T. (1995). Political reform in Mongolia: between Russia and China. Asian Survey, 35(5), 459-471.

96 Tsyrempilov, N.V. (2015). Russian-Qing treaties of the 17th-18th centuries And the status of Tibeto-Mongolian Buddhism in the Russian Empire. Bulletin of the Buryat State University. Pedagogy. Philology. Philosophy, (7).

97 Campi, A. (2006). The rise of cities in nomadic Mongolia. Mongols from country to city: Floating boundaries, pastoralism and city life in the Mongol lands, 21-55.

98 Wanner, M. (2015). Russian-Chinese Trade-in Kyakhta—Trade Development and Volume Indicators 1727–1861. Prague Papers on the History of International Relations, 1, 17-27.

99 Thompstone, S. (1980). Russia's tea traders: a neglected segment of a still neglected entrepreneurial class. Culture, Theory and Critique, 24(1), 131-163.

100 Sántha, I. (2014). Hungarian Witnesses of Infrastructure Construction in Manchuria (1877–1931): The Case of the Eastern Chinese Railway. Inner Asia, 16(1), 152-177.

101 Namsaraeva, S. (2014). Border Language: Chinese Pidgin Russian with a Mongolian 'Accent'. Inner Asia, 16(1), 116-138.

102 Williams, E. T. (1916). The Relations Between China, Russia and Mongolia. American Journal of International Law, 10(4), 798-808.

103 Sanders, A. (1997). Mongolia: Looking to the sea. Geopolitics, 2(1), 134-152.

104 It should be noted that the instrument of bilateral cooperation branches is the representative offices of the Irkutsk, Novosibirsk, Kemerovo regions, the Trans-Baikal Territory, the republics of Buryatia, Altai, Tuva and the city of Moscow, and with Mongol side - consulates general in Irkutsk, Ulan-Ude and Kyzyl, consulate in Elista, as well as the honorary consuls in some Siberian cities.

105 Rygzynov, T. S., & Tsydypov, V. E. (2019, August). The role of international infrastructure projects in sustainable social and economic development of the border areas (the case of Russia and Mongolia). In IOP Conference Series: Earth and Environmental Science (Vol. 320, No. 1, p. 012012). IOP Publishing.

106 Qiang, F., & Bayanjargal, S. (2016). The Study on Trade Policy and Openness of Mongolia: Influences on Trade Flows Between China-Mongolia-Russia (Past and Future). Chinese Business Review, 15(5), 249-264.

107 Humphrey, C. (2015). 'Remote'areas and minoritized spatial orders at the

Russia–Mongolia border. Études mongoles et sibériennes, centrasiatiques et tibétaines, (46).

108 Otgonsaikhan, N. (2015). The Current Situation for Mongolian Foreign Trade and Cooperation with Northeast Asian Countries. ERINA REPORT, 8.

109 Among the Russian regions, the Republic of Buryatia ranks 6th in the volume of exports to Mongolia.

110 Gantuya, D., Imideeva, I., Badaraeva, R., Badaraev, T., Aiyzhy, E., & Liktan, V. (2018). Economy of The Central Asia Region in Conditions Of Globalization (On The Example Of The Republic Of Buryatia, Tuva And Mongolia. International Journal of Management and Business Research, 8(3), 12. Sanders, A. (1997). Mongolia: Looking to the sea. Geopolitics, 2(1), 134-152.

111 In January 2018, at the invitation of the Mayor of Ulaanbaatar, Sundin Batbold, the Inter-parliamentary group of the State Great Khural (VGH) of Mongolia" Russia - Mongolia", with the assistance of the National Trade and Industrialists of Mongolia (NCCI), made a visit with a delegation of businessmen to the Republic of Buryatia. The leadership of the Head of the Republic of Buryatia, Tsydenov, participated in the business conference "Investment potential of the Republic of Buryatia". The business conference was attended by the Ambassador of Russia to Mongolia, Azizov, Deputy Chairman of the Interparliamentary Group "Russia - Mongolia", from the State Great Khural (VGH) of Mongolia Byambasurengiin Ankh-Amgalan, President of the National Chamber of Commerce and Industry of Mongolia Baatarzhavin Lhagwazhav and many others. About 700 people participated in the events, representing more than 40 companies of the Republic of Buryatia, more than 30 companies of Mongolia, and various research institutes of China, Kazakhstan, the Republic of Korea and Germany. The following issues were discussed: supplying electricity to Mongolia, organising transit rail and road transport, developing medical co-operation, tourism, meat supplies from Mongolia.

During the visit, meetings took place between the Head of the Republic of Buryatia, Tsydenov with the President of Mongolia Battulga, Chairman of the Government of Mongolia Ukhnaagiin Khurelsu-khom, Vice-Speaker of the State Great Khural of Mongolia Luvsantseren, members of the Russia-Mongolia Inter-Parliamentary Group, and also Mayor of Ulaanbaatar, Batbold. In April 2018, a delegation of the People's Khural (NH) of the Republic of Buryatia, headed by the Chairman of the National Economy of the Republic of Buryatia, Dorzhiev, visited Mongolia. The deputies got acquainted with the work of the APU group of companies, visited several enterprises, discussed issues of investment cooperation. From 10 to 11 May 2018, a business conference was held in Ulan-Ude for the Republic of Buryatia and Mongolia business people. As part of the event, the Republic heads of approximately 170 companies in Ulaanbaatar visited Buryatia and the aimags of Mongolia working in the field of food, light industry, energy, transport, construction and agriculture. The delegation of Mongolia was headed by a member of the State Great Khural of Mongolia, Chairman, Oyundar, the Secretary of State Ministry of Food, Agriculture and Light Industry of Mongolia, Enkhbat and the Secretary-General of the National Trade and Industry of Mongolia, Oyuuntagsh. Presentations of the economic potential of Mongolia and the Republic were held in Buryatia, meetings of entrepreneurs were organised in the following sections: agro-industrial complexes, transport and logistics complex, industry, medical health and tourism. Also, entrepreneurs of Buryatia and Mongolia held negotiations in a business to business (b2b) format, they made presentations of their enterprises and projects, visited industrial enterprises and organisations of the Republic of Buryatia, including a plywood mill, Baikal fish factory, Selenge factory, confectionery workshop, an enterprise for the installation of automatic gates, "Azhur Tex" a company producing children's knitwear, sports and homeware and hosiery, "Razvivayka", which produces toys and modules, as well as the Buryat Scientific Research Institute of Agriculture. From 7 to 9 June 2018, the delegation of the Republic of Buryatia, led by Deputy Chairman of the Government of the Republic of Buryatia for Economic Development, Zuraev, took part in the forum "Russian-Mongolia 2018 "in Ulaanbaatar. The delegation included trade representatives from the Chamber of Industry of the Republic of Buryatia, Export Center of Buryatia, Fund supporting small businesses and agro-industrial companies.

Within the forum's framework, an exhibition was held with the participation of advanced technologies, equipment products and products of small and medium-sized entrepreneurs in Russia, including from the Republic of Buryatia. Pre-business representatives of the Republic made presentations of their companies and products for Mongolian business people and Mongolian buyers. A workshop "Berezka" was held in Ulan-Ude tasting a line of new cakes produced in Buryatia presented juices, syrups, sea buckthorn jams, herbal teas from Chaga and polymer paving slabs. Following the exhibition, contracts for the supply of manufactured goods in the Republic of Buryatia to Mongolia, negotiations were held with network trading companies about the possibility of supplying food products to Mongolia. At the invitation of the Minister of Food, Agriculture state and light industry of Mongolia, Batzorig, a delegation of the Ministry of Agriculture and Food in the Republic of Buryatia in June 2018 participated in the VIII International Meeting of the Multilateral Partnership on the Global Noah program of sustainable development of animal husbandry in Ulaanbaatar. Within the meeting framework, discussions concerning the supply of meat from Mongolia to the Republic of Buryatia, breeding animals, seedlings, seeds, food products from the Republic of Buryatia in Mongolia, organising fairs and exhibitions of Russian and Mongolian goods took place. In the period from 13 to 16 April 2018 in Irkutsk with the participation of a representative of the Republic of Buryatia, a meeting of the Russian-Mongolian working subgroup scientific support for the development of materials for careful consideration of issues related to the planned construction in Mongolia hydraulic structures in the catchment area of the Selenga took place. At the meeting of the working subgroup, proposals for revision were considered for the districts of Selenga and Lake Baikal in the context of the Shurenskaya hydropower plant construction project and Orkhon hydropower and drainage development projects. According to the meeting results, the parties expressed their readiness to continue discussing projects of hydro-technical structures planned on the Selenga River and its tributaries.

In December 2018, the Regional Development Fund of the Republic of Buryatia in Ulan-Ude held a business conference, "Investor's Day in the Republic of Buryatia", which was attended by entrepreneurs from Mongolia. Concerning regional development with the Republic of Buryatia, negotiations were held with a Mongolian company, APU, on opening a representative office in Buryatia, the establishment of excise warehouse and temporary storage warehouse (TSW). Also, negotiations were held with the Mongolian company TESO on constructing the Teso pasta factory in Buryatia. Work began selecting land plots and premises for the construction or placement of a pasta factory, taking into account the requirements for production. The Regional Development Fund of the Republic of Buryatia focused on implementing the project creation of a cargo handling centre for e-commerce with the involvement of the Mongolian side. In the period 28-29 March 2019 in the Republic of Buryatia, further talks on cooperation between small and medium-sized businesses of Russia and Mongolia, a Russian-Mongolian business mission was held. The Mongolian delegation was actively attended by representatives of various ministries and departments, business communities carrying out tourism, construction, transport and logistics, fish and farming activities.

As part of the Russian-Mongolian business mission, an exhibition fair was held for Mongolian and Russian goods "Baikaltrade 2019", presentations of organisations; business representatives, business contacts exchange and work in sections in the areas of the agro-industrial complex, construction, transport, logistics. Mongolian entrepreneurs visited agricultural enterprises of the Republic, including an industrial park, a jade processing factory, and received advice on compliance with veterinary and phytosanitary supervision requirements. In May 2019, the organisations of the Republic of Buryatia: Ulan-Ude poultry factory, art studio" Dombo ", innovative enterprise "Baikaliya", a chain of stores "Uniform" and others, took part in the International Exhibition of Export and Import Products in Ulaanbaatar. Negotiations with Mongolian companies took place; an agreement was reached on establishing partnerships. As part of the expansion of trade and economic relations of the Republic of Buryatia with Mongolia in the field of agro-industrial complex, the promising directions of cooperation areas are:- expanding the supply of food products from the Republic of Buryatia, Russian Federation to Mongolia;- supplies of breeding material from the Republic of Buryatia to the Russian Federation, walkie-talkies to Mongolia; activation of cooperation between authorised bodies on the issue of lifting restrictions on the import of beef on bones from Mongolia to the Russian Federation; holding an exhibition and fair events in the territories of the Russian Federation and Mongolia; organisation of joint ventures on the territory of the Republic of Buryatia.

112 Khachatryan, N., Schuele, H., Malakshinova, I., & Khachatryan, A. "Chicken and Egg" Problem in the Meat Sector of Buryatia.

113 Biltuev, S., Achituev, V., & Zhamyanov, B. (2019, November). Feeding capacity and meat productivity of sheep of different breeds in the Republic of Buryatia. In IOP Conference Series: Earth and Environmental Science (Vol. 395, No. 1, p. 012115). IOP Publishing.

114 Bouchemla, F., Agoltsov, V. A., Popova, O. M., & Padilo, L. P. (2018). Assessment of the peste des petits ruminants world epizootic situation and estimate its spreading to Russia. Veterinary World, 11(5), 612.

115 Dulguun, A. (2020). To the development of the free economic zone of Mongolia Altanbulag. RSUH/RGGU BULLETIN. Series Economics. Management. Law.

116 Kuklina, M. V., Krasnoshtanova, N. E., Trufanov, A. I., Bogdanov, V. N., & Erdinieva, S. N. (2021). Border area tourism with problems and prospective: RF-Mongolia. In E3S Web of Conferences (Vol. 284, p. 10003). EDP Sciences.

117 Potaev, V., Atanov, N., Subanakov, G., & Tsyrenov, D. (2020). The Russian-Mongolian border zone: a study of the current status and development challenges at the municipal level. Revista Inclusions, 12-19.

118 The Ministry of Foreign Affairs of the Russian Federation. (n.d.) Foreign Minister SERGEY Lavrov's remarks at a joint news conference following talks with

Foreign Minister of Mongolia Batmunkh Battsetseg, Moscow, JUNE 1,2021. Retrieved July 31, 2021, from https://www.mid.ru/en/foreign_policy/news/-/asset_publisher/cKNonkJE02Bw/content/id/4759892

119 ibid.

120 The Ministry of Foreign Affairs of the Russian Federation. (n.d.) Foreign Minister SERGEY LAVROV'S address on RUSSIA'S International activities for Russian Regions' development, delivered at Far Eastern Federal UNIVERSITY (FEFU), and answers to questions from students and Faculty, Vladivostok, July 8, 2021. Retrieved July 31, 2021, from https://www.mid.ru/en/foreign_policy/news/-/asset_publisher/cKNonkJE02Bw/content/id/4809543

121 ibid.

122 Constant, F. (2019). The Legal Administration of Qing Mongolia. Late Imperial China, 40(1), 133-173.

123 Miyawaki, J. (1992). The Chinggisid Principle in Russia. Russian History, 19(1/4), 261-277.

124 Sanders, A. J. (1974). Mongolia: From Sambuu to Tsedenbal. Asian Survey, 971-984.

125 Bayarkhuu, D. (2001). Mongolia and its Third Neighbours. Himalayan and Central Asian Studies, 5(1), 80.

126 Fan, L. (2017). Construction of Russia's "Eurasian Union" and "Economic Corridor among China, Mongolia, and Russia". In China's Belt and Road Initiatives and Its Neighboring Diplomacy (pp. 83-107).

3. Small is Not Vulnerable: India in Mongolia's Third Neighbour Dilemma

Dr RP Pradhan[1]

Abstract

Genghis Khan laid the foundation of the Mongol Empire as one the largest contiguous empires in history. Khan once observed that "with Heaven's aid I have conquered for you a huge empire. But my life was too short to achieve the conquest of the world. That task is left for you". Stretching from Eastern Europe, parts of Central Europe to the Sea of Japan, parts of Arctic, Mongolian empire expanded in the eastward and southward into the Indian subcontinent, mainland South East Asia and the Iranian plateau; and westward as far as the Levant, Carpathian Mountains and to the borders of Northern Europe. It was the second largest empire in history only second to the British Empire.

12th and 13th century Mongolian power and domination were nearly unchallenged. 700 years later, modern Mongolia today is in search of political space, identity and Mongolian experience of autonomy. Squeezed between gigantic Russian territory and ever expanding Chinese domination, Mongolia is in critical search for a 'Third Neighbour' to save Mongolia from the overriding neighbourhood influence. Search for a credible 'Third Neighbour' is a contemporary Mongolian national policy quest.

In the context of Mongolia's 'Third Neighbour Dilemma', this paper examines India as an emerging possible Third Neighbour for Mongolia.

Keywords: Mongol, India, Third Neighbour, Switzerland, Dilemma, Neutrality

Introduction

Mongolia's biggest tryst with destiny is its political geography. Former Prime Minister of Mongolia D. Byambasuren, back in early 1990 had a very appropriate observation on the contemporary Mongolian state and its current geography saying,

"Mongolia is located at the cross roads of three great civilizations, Christian Russia in the North, Confucian China in South and Muslim Central Asia in the West". When we look at the Mongol empire in 13th or 14th century (Fig.1), it was about raw power of domination, bravado and empire on forward march. Beginning with Genghis Khan, Mongolian territory expanded for the next over 200 years. Their territory spread from Eastern Europe, parts of Central Europe to the Sea of Japan and parts of Arctic, Mongolian empire expanded in the eastward and southward into the Indian subcontinent, mainland South East Asia and the Iranian plateau; and westward as far as the Levant, Carpathian Mountains and to the borders of Northern Europe. It was the second largest empire in history only second to the British Empire.

Fig.1 The Grand Mongol Empire in History

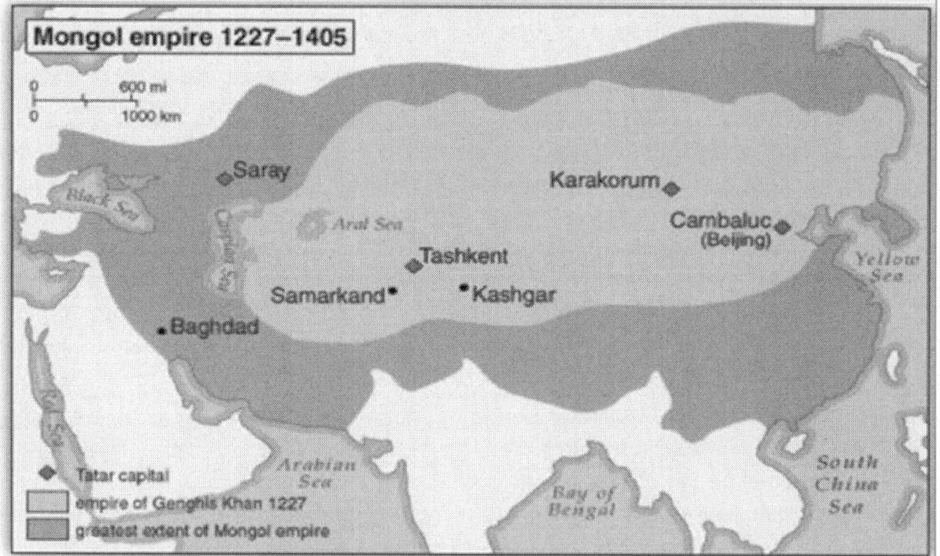

Source: https://www.timewisetraveller.co.uk/genghiskhan.html

13th- 14th century Mongolian power and domination were nearly unchallenged. 700 years later, modern Mongolia today (see Fig.2) is in critical search of political space, identity and Mongolian sense and experience of national autonomy. Squeezed between gigantic Russian territory in the North and ever expanding Chinese domination in South and West, Mongolia is in critical search for a 'Third Neighbour' to hedge Mongolia from the overriding neighbourhood influence. Search for a credible 'Third Neighbour' is a contemporary Mongolian national policy quest. From Japan to European Union and several other political clusters are hotly debated to be Mongolia's possible third neighbour and correspondingly, Mongolia is walking a tight rope to negotiate its diplomacy and foreign policy choices.

Fig.2 Mongolia between China & Russia

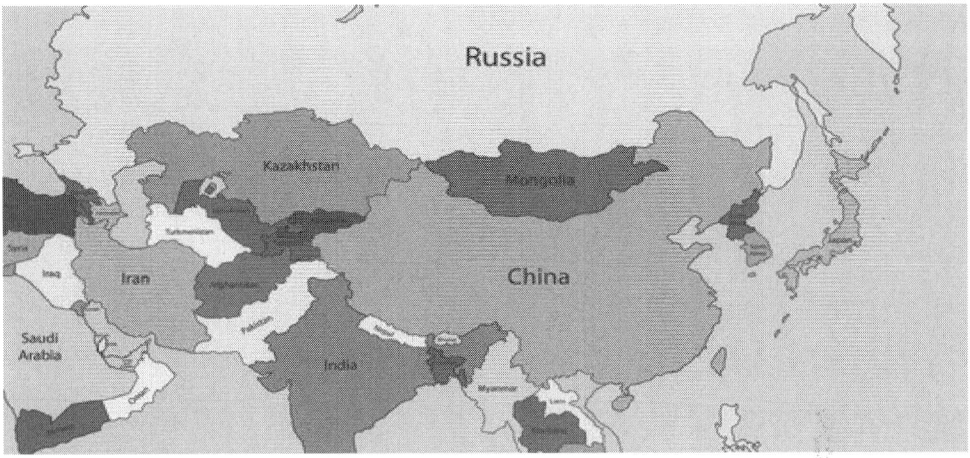

Source: www.goway.com/travel-information/asia/mongolia/geography-and-maps/

While India is geographically located far away, given India's quest to open and expand her contact and engagement into Central Asia, this paper explores the prospect of India playing a possible Third Neighbour for Mongolia opening a small window for Mongolian political aspirations.

Mongol Empire: Reflections from History

Mongolian legendry conquests and spread of Mongolian territory are well documented. Unfortunately however, Mongolian contributions to international system and world development are inadequately written about. Mongolia played a critical role in the Silk Road international trade flow. In order to expand control over Silk Route trade flow, they systematically destroyed Arabian and Turkic cities standing on the southern route prohibiting their commodity exchange control (AlKhateeb, 2017).

During 13th and 15th centuries when successors of Genghis Khan expanded their rule over Central Asia, Iran and the steppes of Eurasia, active Silk Route trade between the East and the West continued to flourish and intensify. The Mongol Golden Horde (the territory from Siberia to Eastern Europe governed by the grandson of Genghis Khan, Berke) with the capital in Serai Berk dominated all over the northern intercontinental caravan road going from China via Otrar and Khoresm, the bottom Volga region, Azov, the Crimea and Europe - the huge part of international trade in the 14th and 15th centuries (Thillaikumar, 2018).

Mongolian political control stimulated the popular caravan trade between China and the Mediterranean countries and several items prominently including sale of silk from China in the European markets flourished (Smith, 2017). Most caravans followed round Transoxiana (ancient name referring to a region and civilization located in lower Central Asia roughly corresponding to modern day eastern Uzbekistan, Tajikistan, southern Kazakhstan and southern Kyrgyzstan), going directly to the Volga to the north from the Caspian Sea, and moved to the Black Sea from here. Khoresm, also called as Greater Khorasan (northeast province of Greater Iran) was the southern sector of that northern route that continued to play the role of the link in the chain of regional and intercontinental goods exchange. Urgench (a city in present Uzbekistan) was another major center of trade whose markets witnessed great trade flow. Conscious of trade flow and its corresponding profits, the Mongols actively maintained and protected the trade corridor; making it safe for trade relations flowing to and fro the East and the West practicing liberal trade and taxation policies while ensuring bribery, mal trade practice and bureaucracy are under check (Morgan D. , 2009).

Thus, connecting Europe and Asia, the Mongolian empire served as a land bridge between the two continents while maintaining effective chain of relay, watch and communication centers for communications and trade flow purposes. Mongolian empire also promoted interfaith tolerance of divergent faiths and religions, and established inviolability of the special status of the emperor's envoys. In the 13th and 14th centuries the lands of the Mongol Empire were under the Pax Mongolica that provided peace and safe travel within the empire and contributed to free and safe trade through the Silk Road. In the 13th and 14th centuries, Mongols ruled parts of Russia and China. However, by the mid-14th century, the empire started developing fissures and gradually to disintegrated.

The Mongol empire, the largest contiguous land empire in history and second largest to British Empire in size, served as a critical trade, culture and civilization linkage bridge and meeting point between Europe and Asia that in turn, promoted confluence civilizations. Acting as a link and catalyst empire, Pax Mongolica, if we can call it, provided political stability as a means to safe travel within the empire and contributed to free and safe trade through the Silk Road corridor (Jargalsaikhan, 2018).

During 13th and 14th centuries, Mongolians ruled parts of present day Russia and China. However, by the mid-14th century, the mammoth empire started slackening and incrementally started to disintegrate (Morgan D. , 2009). Russian territory expanded to the east while China started to move west and north, squeezing gradually the loose ends of the Mongol empire. After the collapse of the Mongolian Yuan dynasty (Yuan dynasty first emperor was famous Kublai Khan) that ruled China; Mongols retreated altogether to their homeland, north of the Great Wall of China. Several Chinese rebellions and weak Mongolian governance finally ended

Mongolian control over Chinese territories (Zeidan, 2020). Towards the end of the 17th century, Russian expansion had reached well into the lands of the Mongols (Jargalsaikhan, 2018). As the corona virus has been bothersome to the health and economy of the world today, 'Black Death', apparently emanating from Gobi desert area and traveling through silk route corridor of Mongolia, seemed to have caused devastating loss to human life, trade and economy as well as causing lasting blows to the Mongolian empire too. As we see from hindsight understanding, among several other reasons, 'Black Death' or 'Bubonic Plague' as it was called, could well be traced to the Mongol Empire and Pax Mongolica, which provided safe travel of the diseasethrough the Silk Road that otherwise had facilitated transportation of goods and services and prosperity also became the final nail in the down fall of great Mongol empire (Shipman, 2014).

Today Mongolia is territorially, culturally and in terms of political and religious identity and persuasion is fully squeezed between Russia, China and Central Asia. Standing at a crossroad of cultures and contemporary political designs and ambitions of sphere of influence, Mongolia indeed is facing the heat of Samuel Huntington's 'Clash of Civilization' and its existential threats.

Mongolia's Neighbourhood Dilemma

Being a small country next to a big one is tragedy enough. Mongolia unfortunately has two very powerful countries of the world as its immediate neighbour. The challenge correspondingly is bound to be manifold. As we analyze Mongolia's neighbourhood to capture the tiny country's predicament, it is necessary to explain and simplify the depth of Mongolia's neighbourhood challenges.

Mongolia, at the peak of Pax Mongolica had an almost unending empire. If we simplify Pax Mongolica size in modern parlance of nation-states, Mongolian territory expanded over 30 countries of today's world with a population of around 3 billion people. Present day Mongolia is just the opposite of its historical past and sobered down in almost all ways.

Corresponding to the rise of China, it is now been a time for military muscleman ship in many parts of the world. Be it Indo-Pacific or Tibetan heights or even the interiors of Russia, there is a huge unilateral and joint-multilateral defense exercises all over the world. MALABAR to Milan and Sea Guardian to Russian Victory parade in June last year, several joint defense exercises try and communicate that the changing international order is anything but volatile.

Last year June 24, Russia celebrated victory parade with grandeur. The 2020 Victory Day Parade in Moscow took place in a spectacular way in Moscow's Red Square on 24 June 2020. It was to commemorate two goals – first, the '75th Diamond

Jubilee' of the capitulation of Nazi Germany in the Second World War in 1945 and second, to revisit the historic Moscow Victory Parade of 1945. Defense forces from twenty countries participated in the parade including Mongolia, Armenia, Belarus, Serbia, and Uzbekistan. Even India joined the event to reconsolidate India-Russia friendly ties.

Though Mongolia officially participated in the Victory Parade, several things went wrong and Ulaanbaatar, even after joining the event became in the receiving end of Russian wrath. On the same day, Mongolia was to hold Mongolia's regular, democratic parliamentary elections. As a result of Mongolian national election code of conduct and in order to project electoral neutrality, Mongolian state television (MNB), in the last moment decided not to telecast the live parade in Mongolia. Putin had visited Ulaanbaatar in the previous year and had signed "Permanent Treaty of Friendship" with his Mongolian counterpart President Khaltmaagiin Battulga indicating a state of bilateral friendship and mutuality. At the time of the signing of the treaty, Putin stressed on the importance of the "political, economic and cultural" relationship between Russia and Mongolia (Hussain, 2020).

When the Mongolian National Broadcaster (MNB) last moment scrapped the plans to live broadcast the Red Square Victory Parade, the Russian Embassy at Ulaanbaatar openly criticized this decision in a rather ill tempered Face book page public post, accusing MNB of an "aberration of vision" and even subservience to Western interests. May be inadvertently or otherwise, the MNB board of directors joined ... a whole campaign of accusing and counter accusations of Russian electoral interference nearly everywhere in the world" (Radchenko, 2020).

The remarks caused a storm of controversy. MNB Director Luvsandashiin Ninjjamts in a letter to Russian Ambassador Iskander Azizov, called the embassy's remarks "clearly insulting" and demanded an official apology. Mongolia has seen it all and Mongolia-Moscow interface has never been mutual nor respectful. Sanjaagiin Bayar, former Mongolian Prime Minister who had also served as Mongolia's ambassador in Russia, connected the Russian embassy's outburst to the old practice of Soviet ambassadors trying to dictate to their foreign host governments what they should and should not do.

Mongolians know firsthand how Soviet Union intervened in Mongolian affairs. The country became a Soviet satellite two decades before the same ill fate were extended to Central and Eastern European countries. In the 1930s, the Soviets and their Mongolian puppets, the Mongolian People's Revolutionary Party (MPRP) initiated a policy of purging, very often called as 'Great Purging'. The policy was unhesitant in slaughtering tens of thousands of people in anti religious campaigns and waves of political repression which continues to remain vivid in Mongolian political psyche even to this day.

Mongolia has witnessed two sets of political leaders. One set were nationalists and had their Mongolia identity close to their heart. Mongolian Prime Minister Peljidiin Genden and Anandyn Amar belonged to this set of political leaders who had to sacrifice their life for the national pride of Mongolia. The other set of leaders like Khorloogiin Choibalsan and Yumjaagiin Tsedenbal were all overly ready to toe the Soviet line.

It is in this cross currents of Mongolian nationalism and personal political ambition, the celebrated victims were Mongolian Prime Minister Peljidiin Genden. Genden had the nerve to publicly quarrel with Joseph Stalin. Peljidiin Genden seems to have smashed the Soviet dictator's smoking pipe to pieces in one nasty altercation in a party hosted in Ulaanbaatar. It was no mean offence. Genden was sent to Moscow and executed in 1937. His successor, Anandyn Amar, suffered a similar fate too. Amar was arrested, sent to the Soviet Union, and executed there in 1941 (Radchenko, 2020).

These political events led to the *de facto* premiership of Khorloogiin Choibalsan, also known as Mongolia's Stalin. Choibalsan was more than willing and submitted himself to serving Soviet aims and objectives in Asia. Ivan Ivanov, the then Soviet plenipotentiary in Ulaanbaatar closely collaborated and supervised Choibalsan. It was on Khorloogiin Choibalsan's and Ivanov's close supervision and strategy that Mongolia willingly got involved in the Soviet war efforts during the 1940s. Mongolia even sent nearly half a million horses (which proved their resilience on the front line) and sponsored a tank brigade to bolster several of the Russian conspiratorial missions. Though Mongolia is working out to gain Japanese support today as a part of its third neighbour strategy, back then, Mongolia also joined the Soviets in fighting the Japanese in Manchuria in August 1945 (Radchenko, 2020).

Choibalsan's successor, Yumjaagiin Tsedenbal, was even more anxious to enlist himself to his Soviet masters and repeatedly requested Mongolia's annexation to the Soviet Union. Fortunately for the nationalist Mongolians, Soviet Union refused complete annexation for some strange reasons. Tsedenbal also fought Moscow's case tirelessly in Beijing during the unfolding of Sino-Soviet doctrinal split in early 1960s. Apparently, in December 1962, in a conversation with the Chinese Premier Zhou Enlai, his ardent defense of Soviet policies got so charged and explosive that both of them nearly came to blows.

Mongolia has gone through many phases of political upheaval. Now in the last over two decades, corresponding to the disintegration of Soviet Union and economic meltdown in Russia, China has been an ever ambitious player in the region. While the international order is experiencing the impact of China's rise which Professor Graham Allison paraphrased as phenomena of 'Thucydides Trap', Mongolia and Central Asia like the regions in South China Sea (SCS) are experiencing the immediate similar heat of Chinese rough ride in their domestic affairs. Starting from Chinese goods and services flooding their domestic markets to big and lucrative construction project contracts and China's ambitious revival of Silk Road and Belt and Road (BRI) project, the entire region has come under China's immediate sphere of influence. While the Russian's called Mongolia as their 'near periphery', China in all its actions and domination feels that the region is only a territorial extension of China.

Mongolia is wholly caught between the devil and the Dead Sea. Added to the Mongolian political woes, Buddhist Mongolia is also at the cross roads of Christian Russia, Confucian China and Muslim Central Asia converting the woes into a formidable depth of Samuel Huntington's 'Clash of Civilization' in its grandeur manifestation.

In the context of Mongolian contemporary predicament, Mongolia has very actively explored a third neighbour option in its foreign policy choices. Sometimes European Union or Eastern European countries and other times exploring Japan as a possible third neighbour, Mongolia is going through this policy quest judiciously. Mongolia has also tried to ply between Russia and China to carve out its own political space. Mongolia has also imagined involving Washington or joining NATO as a third neighbour option. Third Neighbour policy therefore is a genuine official ongoing position and quest in Mongolia which has not yielded any assuring benefit as yet. The country therefore is open to series of third neighbours who possibly can supplant Mongolian sense of political insecurity. India is one such candidate in Mongolian foreign policy choices.

Mongolian Recourses: Boon or Bane?

Resources are supposed to be national assets for economic growth. Given Mongolia's mineral resources, both Russia and China are also equally provoked to carve out a sphere of influence in the tiny country of roughly 3 million people. Apart from geography, as Mongolian intellectual Batbayar Baatarkhuu would put it, Mongolia's wealth is the country's second curse too (Baatarkhuu, 2020). IMF identifies Mongolia as the 29th resource rich developing country in the world. One of the World Bank study theorizes resource abundance and economic growth correlation to sum up that there is no empirical correlation. Instead the report concludes with empirical evidence that resourcefulness has very often led to resource mismanagement (World Bank, 2006). Diamonds have not made Angola rich. Oil has not delivered prosperity to Venezuela. Rich reserves of copper, gold, diamonds, cobalt, uranium, Colton and oil have fed and funded wars in the Democratic Republic of Congo (DRC). In Russia, a few oligarchs have gained immense wealth, while 70% of Russians earn less than $380 per month (World Bank, 2006).

Caught in the limitations of geography and huge mineral resources like oil, gold, silver, iron, coal, copper, molybdenum, tungsten, phosphates, tin, nickel, zinc, and fluorspar, Mongolia has naturally been an attractive destination initially for Russia and now for China. Unlike Switzerland, since the country also witnesses' political corruption, critical economic assets and contracts pertaining to their extraction are also subject to bribery practices converting Mongolia, like most developing countries, to remain vulnerable too.

Small States Security Vulnerability: Normative Explanations

"Poor Mexico, so far from God and yet so close to the US" - is a popular Mexican saying (Carroll, 2017). Young and old, all Mexicans are very aware of the depth of this saying. Former President of Mexico, Porfirio Díaz very regrettably observed this some 150 years ago and the saying continues even today. Geography has been Mexico's biggest bane. Back in 1846, Mexico ceded territory to Americans in the Rio Grande war and Mexican territories like present day Arizona, California, New Mexico, Texas, Colorado, Nevada, and Utah constituting nearly 55% of Mexican territory were ceded to the United States (Carroll, 2017).

Back in 1926, three American mariners while cruising in the Gulf of Mexico apparently strayed into the Mexican territorial waters. The mariners were quickly arrested by Mexican authorities. The Americans were so furious that they demanded apology from the Mexican government. Though Mexico initially resisted, finally it so happened that Mexico had to officially apologize and as though it was not enough, Mexico had to pay a twenty-one gun salute to the American flag. For the generations of Mexicans, history has always been troublesome and too humiliating.

In the context of Mexican geographic proximity to the Americans and successive American high handedness, there is yet another popular slogan in Mexico that says "you have taken our land and we will populate it". Given Mexican domestic economic development challenges, crossing over to the American side is almost like a Mexican national sport. Somehow, young Mexicans have to sneak into the American territory. Strange as it may appear, most of Southern States of USA today have more than 60% Mexican population who have sneaked over.

Unlike Mongolia, Mexico is not land locked nor is it a vulnerable state. Instead, Mexico is a rising economic power and since 1994, Mexico has forged NAFTA- a free trade agreement with USA and Canada which has seen many American jobs vanishing to Mexico. Ever since NAFTA was signed, several mainland American industries have moved their bases to USA-Mexico border to take advantage of Mexican cheaper labour force. While this has caused American job loss, it has created what is known as Maquiladora Traders- a term in Spanish referring to border traders.

Mexico has somewhat taken revenge of their humiliation and it is an American requirement to halt Mexicans entering into their territory. Instruments like NAFTA are yet another method through which small states may reconstruct their engagement paradigm. Unfortunately however, Mongolian market and economy are already deluged initially by Russians and now by Chinese and free trade instrument option is neither available to Mongolia nor advisable either.

While Mexicans handled and continue to handle their vulnerability in variety of ways, normatively, most countries in the world small or big are vulnerable in many ways. In spite of India being a very large country and a nuclear power, Indian vulnerability is critical and very large too. Choked between Pakistan sponsored Islamic terrorism and rising Chinese ambition of territorial aggrandizement, India indeed is negotiating a difficult power balance which can unfold into a major war. Japan also faces similar predicament of Chinese rise and sphere of influence. Such predicaments are there for almost every country in variety of formats and intensity. Each nation therefore has to evolve its own mechanism of security suitable for itself. It can be soft diplomacy to security coalition as well as trade cooperation and many such modules. Argentina and Brazil had mostly been opposed to each other and in search of regional hegemony. Located between them are tiny Paraguay and Uruguay who felt the pinch of Brazil-Argentina rivalry. However, the free trade agreement of MERCOSUR in 1990s softened the political climate for all of them.

Negotiating Vulnerability: Mongolian Options

Easier said than done, Mongolian choices indeed are limited. However, there are several choices and options and several evidences around the world are available too where number of countries have handled their vulnerability in variety of ways.

Case of Djibouti: Djibouti- the horn of Africa and one of the smallest country in Africa and vulnerable in all dimensions and perspective is a great case example today where several countries from across the world are trying their foothold in search of political designs. A former colony of France, today Djibouti is open to any country to use Djibouti's land even for defense purposes. France has a naval base in Djibouti under a bilateral agreement and 5000 troops are stationed that also includes German and Spanish soldiers (Igrouane, 2019). The United States has also leased a Naval base 'Camp Lemonnier'- US Naval Expeditionary Base, situated next to Djibouti - Ambouli International Airport in Djibouti City, and houses a Combined Joint Task Force (Simon, 2020). The British are also using the American base for surveillance purposes. Corresponding to the rise of China and the intensifying geopolitical challenges in the Indo-Pacific Region (IPR), host of countries today have already opened their defense bases in Djibouti and the lease revenue is now a source of major revenue earning for Djibouti. China and Japan have already leased and opened their naval and air force base in Djibouti and Saudi Arab is in line to explore a defense base in Djibouti. China is expanding fast and wide in most part of Africa with huge seaport, dams and several other construction, mining and energy projects. The Chinese People's Liberation Army (PLA) Support Base in Djibouti is a new strategic frontier for China in the Horn of Africa. China began constructing its first PLA's overseas base at Djibouti's Doraleh Port in March 2016 (Bhat, 2020). China is also building and developing seaport facilities in Djibouti. Japan similarly has opened an air force base in Djibouti since 2009 (Ryall, 2018).

Given the pluralisation of defense bases and forces in Djibouti, while the regional influence of Djibouti has expanded, it also becomes a larger neutralizing platform for the critically opposing powers and forces like US and Japan with that of China.

Swiss Neutrality & Lessons

Europe has been the most conflict ridden in most part of history both within and outside of Europe. In the midst of raging conflicts and institutionalized colonization policies and European powers highhanded political and economic rough ride in most part of the world, Switzerland serves as a unique case example of militarized neutrality – a prize position rarely possible and serves as a case example for all the small nations of the world including Mongolia. Land locked like Mongolia and located well within the middle of Germany, France, Italy and Austria, Swaziland in fact inherits the geographic liability and provocations of all possible wars. Yet, learning from Europe's culture and regime of conflict and their own defeat from France, Switzerland has learnt to maintain a state of neutrality is no mean achievement. The greater lesson from Swiss neutrality emerges from its evolution to be a peace buffer and place of peace negotiation and diplomacy not for Europe alone but for the international community as a whole.

Switzerland is not the only neutral country in the world. Countries like Ireland, Austria and Costa Rica also follow some degree of noninterventionist approach in many ways (Andrews, 2018). However, Switzerland curiously remains the oldest and most respected neutral nation in the world today. Five years ago, in November 2016, Switzerland celebrated five hundred years of policy of neutrality. Even during both the World Wars, Switzerland was able to be cautiously neutral (Mclaughlin, 2016).

Switzerland's earliest move toward neutrality goes back to 1515, when the Swiss Confederacy suffered a devastating loss to the French at the Battle of Marignano. Following the defeat, the Confederacy abandoned its expansionist policies and looked to avoid future conflict in the interest of self-preservation (Andrews, 2018). Switzerland came under the radar of Napoleonic Wars. France invaded Switzerland in 1798 and converted the tiny nation as a French satellite empire, forcing the small nation to compromise its neutrality. However, soon after Napoleon's Waterloo defeat, major European powers wisely and in the interest of regional peace and stability, concluded infavour of a neutral Swiss confederation. Neutral Switzerland could serve as a valuable buffer zone between France and Austria and contribute to regional stability and peace negotiations (Jesse, 2014). Two hundred years ago, Switzerland was acknowledged as a neutral state in the Treaty of Paris. Even Vienna Congress in 1815 recognized Swiss neutrality while League of Nations, formally recognized Switzerland's neutrality on Feb. 13, in 1920.

Post Second World War; while Switzerland continued to remain fiercely neutral in regard to military affairs, the country has taken more active role in international affairs through foreign aid and humanitarian assistance initiatives. It has never joined the North Atlantic Treaty Organization (NATO) or the European Union, and only joined the United Nations in 2002. Despite its longstanding neutrality, the country still maintains a smart army of around 600,000 soldiers for defense purposes. While neutrality is Switzerland's political value, position and culture, Swiss nationals (all males between the ages of 18 and 34) however, are required to render part-time military service and Swiss army is considered a very smart army who can be mobilized very quickly for eventualities.

Mongolia has a great lesson to learn from Swiss neutrality experience. Given Switzerland's prominent international banking regime, and the country as a hub of international diplomacy and peace negotiations, geographically vulnerable countries can take great queue from Swiss experience.

Lessons from Singapore

Singapore serves as yet another example of economic wonders out of a small fishing village in South East Asia. Lee Kuan Yew, the founding father of one of Asia's smallest but most developed economies, died in March 2015. Lee Kuan Yew, the statesman who transformed Singapore from a small port city into a wealthy global hub truly served the best of Singapores national interest. After its separation from Malaysia in 1965, Lee led Singapore with vision and astuteness to develop it as one of the world's most powerful financial centers (Ketchell, 2015).

As per IMF assessment, Singapore's main industry was manufacturing at the time of independence. However, with the rise of modern seaport led economy and Singapore's service sector, its GDP per capita growth rate under Lee's leadership reached to be one of the highest in 2013, just behind oil-rich Qatar and private banking centre Luxembourg. A mixed population profile of Chinese, Malaysian and Indian heritage, Singapore's economic development could well have been a casualty of ethnic turmoil. Under the leadership of Lee, Singapore opted for the creation of a rule based state and capitalized on a port based economic development model facilitated under a political climate of efficiency and growth. National University of Singapore (NUS), National Technical University (NTU) as well as Lee Kuan Yew Institute of Public Policy are some of the finest academic institutions of the world which further highlight the structural, human capital and efficiency focus of Singapore's nation building process. Net result, Singapore port does more business today than all the seaports of India could jointly imagine.

Singapore flourished on the inherited advantages and foresightedness of Lee to transform into the ranks of New York, London and Switzerland as a global financial hub. As a key port during the British Empire, Singapore was in a strong position for trading activity. Since Singapore had no other resources other than their natural port asset and location of Singapore right on the middle of maritime highways of the world, Lee built on this and the result is there for everybody to see (Bhaskaran, 2018).

Lee has been criticized by many for authoritarianism that stifled political dissent and press freedoms. However, his firm grip on power and foresight, corruption free financial practices and maintenance of political stability served the country's economic growth objectives very well. The orderliness that Singapore is known for today provided structural attractiveness to foreign investments and billions of dollar poured into the country, ensuring the country's success.

Mongolia lacks this structural vision and orientation. Mongolian leadership needs to learn from Lee Kuan Yew's model to examine the politico-economic grow path for Mongolia.

India in Mongolia's Third Neighbour Dilemma

Geographically India is located well away from Mongolia for any possible immediate good neighbourly involvement and engagement. Forcing India to be a political savior of Mongolia's neighbourhood woes shall therefore suffer from serious bias of over extrapolation. Additionally, India's land connectivity to Central Asia continuously meeting Pakistan's spoil sport diplomacy, India's active role in Central Asia and Mongolia is structurally limited. Yes, Chabahar port deal with Iran in 2016 indeed opened India's glimmer of hope and prospect of India's maritime connectivity via Chabahar port and Afghanistan. However, now Afghanistan is almost in the doorstep of Talibanism ruling the roost, the civil war torn Afghanistan is in tatters which by default shatters India's Central Asia dream. Iran under American sanction has also posed additional problem for India. In a climate of sanction and strategic threat, Iran has been more and more cozying up with China which further complicates India's future in the region. India's Central Asia score card is more with negative points and unfavourable strategic equations than any assuring developments.

Nevertheless, in a globalised international order of today, there is a good case for India-Mongolia engagement which can well qualify towards Mongolian third neighbour dilemma analysis. In the context of India's Act East Policy (AEP) and Indo-Central Asian growing engagement focus, Mongolia strategically figures as an extended neighbourhood for India's foreign policy scheme of things (Soni, 2016).

India and Mongolia share one of the finest bilateralism today. India established diplomatic relations with Mongolia as far back as December 1955. India was the first country outside the Eastern Bloc to establish diplomatic relations with Mongolia. India supported Mongolia in having UN and NAM memberships. In 2015, both countries marked their 60th anniversary of establishment of diplomatic relations which itself is a mile stone. Since then, there have been treaties of mutual friendship and cooperation between the two countries in 1973, 1994, 2001 and 2004.

Culturally and historically, India and Mongolia have interacted since antiquity through the powerful vehicle of Buddhism that emanated from India in late 6th century BC. According to number of Mongolian scholars, Buddhism traveled to Mongolia through the Tibetan highlands. During the Hunnu State of 3rd century BC, and later during the period of Pax Mongolica, Buddhist monks and several traders from India visited Mongolia. While Nalanda University has been a historical meeting point, most Mongols consider India as the holy land of Buddha.

India currently is in the process of developing Ramayan and Buddhism corridor for cultural and religious tourism economy to prosper. If these corridors take shape, in the times to come, the entire Buddhist community spread in Sri Lanka to South East Asia and Far East as well as China and Mongolian Buddhist religious imaginations and orientation may trigger great amount of travel, transport and range of interactions in the socio-religious front.

Though history and culture has gained greater currency and relevance as instruments of Joseph Nye's Soft Power Diplomacy', they are nevertheless, long distance instruments and more so in the case of Indo-Mongolian Bohemism.

In the last few years however, both countries have bilaterally made great head ways. In April-May 2016, both countries had a joint military exercise with counter insurgency as focus (Parameswaran, 2016). While it could no way be called as a power display, nevertheless, it displayed a degree Indo-Mongolian meeting of minds.

In the process of a three nation tour of China, Mongolia and South Korea, Indian Prime Minister Narendra Modi landed in Mongolia on May 17th 2015. It was a historic visit as no other Indian Prime Minister had ever visited Mongolia before. Prime Minister Modi's visit to Mongolia opened new chapter in India-Mongolia relations. Modi himself twitted that Mongolia is an integral part of India's Act East Policy (AEP). If we expand India's rising focus in Central Asia and Mongolia, it is more in the context of China's squeezing India in Indian periphery through 'String of Pearls' and Beijing's ambitious US$8 trillion Belt and Road Initiative (BRI). Reaching to Central Asia and Mongolia, India, in a limited scale though, is trying to work around China's periphery for strategic counter balance.

Following Prime Minister Modi's visit to Mongolia, India extended a US$1billion credit line to Mongolia for the construction of Mongol Petrochemical refinery project. India's State-run Engineers India Ltd (EIL) is extending project management consultancy for the development of the oil refinery near Sainshand in southern Dornogovi province in Mongolia which is expected to be be commissioned by December 2022 (PTI, 2019). The refinery is projected to meet about 75% of Mongolia's oil requirement. India is also involved in the construction of roads, railways and power line for the refinery. India has taken lead in solar power tapping and International Solar Alliance (ISA) development. Responding to Indian invitation, Mongolia has requested for ISA membership.

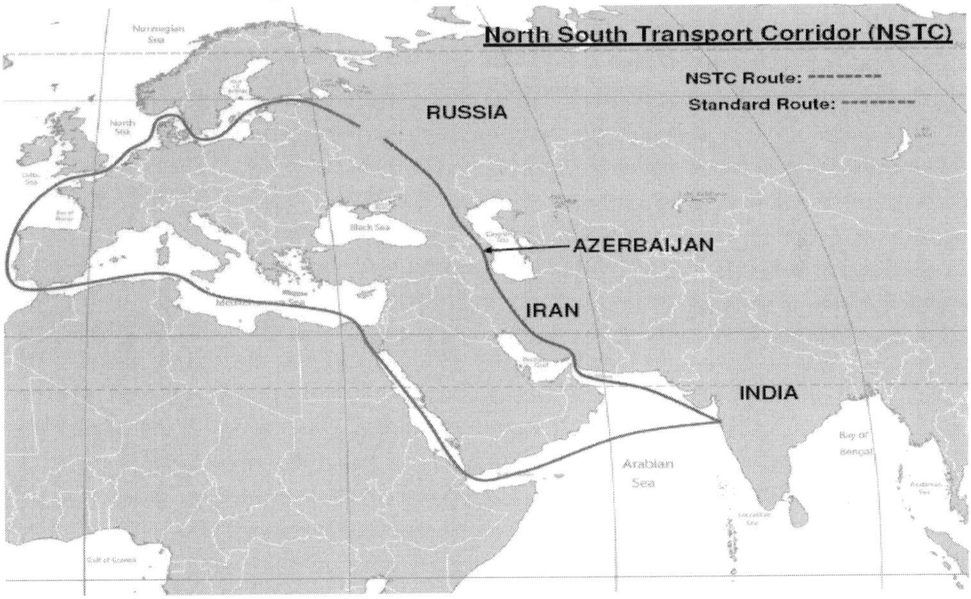

While India's engagement with Mongolia in quantitative terms is rather limited, given the fresh bilateral involvement and India's growing desire to play more creative role in the region, Mongolia can well configure India as one of the third neighbour. India is also exploring greater role in Central Asia through Chabahar port and Afghanistan. Additionally, India is also approaching the Central Asian region through International North-South Transport Corridor as well as Russia-India Corridor as well as Chennai-Vladivostok Eastern Maritime Corridor. Given the great infrastructure diplomacy China initiated for the first time as almost like a weapon of connectivity and influence paddling, several alternative proposals are emerging as China countering infrastructure initiatives. Road, rail and sea connectivity promising more international trade and movement of goods and services, regional conflicts are also likely to be pushed under the carpet or negotiated through diplomatic modes. However, greater transport and trade movement shall demand economic efficiency for each country.

Though Mongolia is not directly connected through these infrastructure projects but more linked to China's BRI, it is obvious that there will be more and more trade movement. While trade has potential to soften political climate, Mongolia being a mineral resource rich country, internationalization of Mongolian extraction wealth may also work as a catalyst for Mongolia to negotiate with its neighbours.

Conclusion

Being located between Russian Federation and China, while geography has been the biggest present day predicament of Mongolia, Samuel Huntington's 'Clash of Civilization' seems more in real manifestation in Mongolia making the tiny Asian Republic more vulnerable. While clash of civilizations is a net reality for Mongolia today and Joseph Nye's 'Soft Power' diplomacy seem the only option and way out, the weapons of soft power diplomacy appear too soft for Mongolia to address Mongolian predicament of dealing with two most powerful and ambitious nations of the world as its neighbours. Russia and China are global powers of serious consequence. Since the entire international political system and international order is deeply feeling the weight of Russia and China's ambitious and often dominating and coercing foreign policy mechanism, Mongolia has no immediate choice than to negotiate friendly ties with both of them for its existential reasons.

However, as discussed earlier, small states like Switzerland, Singapore or even Djibouti have tried and experimented with neutrality, hard core text book prescribed development models or opened them to internationalization like the case of Djibouti; Mongolia may have to try many such modules to safeguard Mongolian national interest and pride.

Additionally, Mongolia could well be internationalized in many ways. Like NUS or NTU, Mongolia can think of high repute International Universities and institutions attracting international students and professors. It can also, like Switzerland, open international banking. Even internationalizing Mongolian tourism sector to attract substantial international visitors could well expand Mongolian national image from being a land locked country to an international destination. Internationalization helps internally to develop and upgrade local skill while it creates an expanded profile for the nation. Such platforms are revenue earning instruments too.

Mongolian third neighbour dilemma is a political policy quest. Since India and Mongolia are willing, it makes a good case for consolidating the engagement further. Additionally, India is seen as a civilizational country with very positive and peace centric orientation and foreign policy practices. While China's rise has virtually ruptured international power balance, it is the rise of India as a counter balance is an assuring proposition. As the international order is experiencing more and more transition driven teething problems, contestations and conflict, India is seen and analyzed as a credible swing state that has the ability, orientation and desire for peace options. Mongolia may not be misplaced to configure India as a credible friend, well-wisher and a well-meaning third neighbour.

References

AlKhateeb, F. (2017, June 23). Remembering Mongol invasion and destructions of Baghdad. *Egypt Today*. Retrieved July 13, 2021, from https://www.egypttoday.com/Article/4/8673/Remembering-Mongol-invasion-and-destructions-of-Baghdad

Andrews, E. (2018, Aug 22). Why is Switzerland a neutral country? *History*. Retrieved Aug 13, 2021, from https://www.history.com/news/why-is-switzerland-a-neutral-country

Baatarkhuu, B. (2020, Summer). *How can Mongolia Avoid the Resource Curse?* Syracuse University. Retrieved Aug 14, 2021, from https://surface.syr.edu/eli/58/

Bhaskaran, M. (2018). *Getting Singapore in shape: Economic challenges and how to meet them.* Lowy Institute. Retrieved Aug 14, 2021, from https://www.lowyinstitute.org/publications/getting-singapore-shape-economic-challenges-and-how-meet-them-0

Bhat, V. (2020). *Construction fast-tracked at China PLA's first overseas base in Djibouti.* New Delhi: India Today. Retrieved July 13, 2021, from https://www.indiatoday.in/world/story/construction-fast-tracked-at-china-pla-s-first-overseas-base-in-djibouti-1736703-2020-10-30

Carroll, R. (2017). *So far from God, so close to the US': Mexico's troubled past with its neighbour.* London: The Guardian . Retrieved Aug 04, 2021, from https://www.theguardian.com/us-news/2017/feb/01/donald-trump-us-mexico-relations-history

Hussain, S. (2020, June 23). Why Is Russia Moving Closer to Mongolia? *The Diplomat*. Retrieved Aug 14, 2021, from https://thediplomat.com/2020/06/why-is-russia-moving-closer-to-mongolia/

Igrouane, Y. (2019). *Djibouti: A Busy Hub of Foreign Military Bases on the Horn of Africa.* Inside Arabia. Retrieved July 13, 2021, from https://insidearabia.com/djibouti-a-busy-hub-of-foreign-military-bases-on-the-horn-of-africa/

Jargalsaikhan, E. (2018, Oct 19). The Role of Small States in Promoting International Security: The Case of Mongolia. *Journal for Peace and Nuclear Disarmament, 1*(2), 404-435. Retrieved July 12, 2021, from https://www.tandfonline.com/doi/full/10.1080/25751654.2018.1526628

Jesse, J. D. (2014). Swiss Neutrality Examined: Model, Exception or Both? *Journal of Military and Strategic Studies, 15*(3), 60-83. Retrieved Aug 14, 2021, from https://jmss.org/article/download/58112/43729

Ketchell, M. (2015). *How Lee Kuan Yew transformed Singapore from small town into global financial hub.* The Conversation Media Group Ltd. Retrieved Aug 14, 2021, from https://theconversation.com/how-lee-kuan-yew-transformed-singapore-from-small-town-into-global-financial-hub-39192

Mclaughlin, W. (2016, Sep 12). The Battle Of Marignano: The Reason For (Almost) 500 Years Of Swiss Neutrality. *War History Online*. Retrieved Aug 14, 2021, from https://www.warhistoryonline.com/history/battle-marignano-reason-almost-500-years-swiss-neutrality.html

Morgan, D. (2009, Sep 09). The Decline and Fall of the Mongol Empire. *Journal Of The Royal Asiatic Society, 19*(04), 427 - 437. doi:https://doi.org/10.1017/S1356186309990046

Morgan, D. (2009, Oct). The Decline and Fall of the Mongol Empire. *Journal of the Royal Asiatic Society, 19*(4), 427-437 . Retrieved July 12, 2021, from https://www.jstor.org/stable/27756097

Parameswaran, P. (2016, April 28). India, Mongolia Launch Military Exercise With Counterterrorism Focus. *The Diplomat*. Retrieved Aug 15, 2021, from https://thediplomat.com/2016/04/india-mongolia-launch-military-exercise-with-counterterrorism-focus/

PTI. (2019). *India-funded oil refinery in Mongolia to be completed by 2022-end.* New Delhi: Business Standard. Retrieved Aug 16, 2021, from https://www.business-standard.com/article/pti-stories/india-funded-oil-refinery-in-mongolia-to-be-completed-by-2022-end-pradhan-119092001148_1.html

Radchenko, S. (2020, June 26). Russia Wants to Keep Mongolia in Its Place. *Foreign Policy*. Retrieved Aug 14, 2021, from https://foreignpolicy.com/2020/06/26/russia-putin-mnb-wants-to-keep-mongolia-in-its-place/

Ryall, J. (2018). *Japan to expand Djibouti base despite decline in piracy.* Berlin: DW News. Retrieved July 13, 2021, from https://www.dw.com/en/japan-to-expand-djibouti-base-despite-decline-in-piracy/a-46356825

Shipman, P. L. (2014, Nov-Dec). The Bright Side of the Black Death. *American Scientist, 102*(6), p. 410. doi:10.1511/2014.111.410

Simon, S. (2020). *Why are there so many military bases in Djibouti?* Medium. Retrieved July 13, 2021, from https://medium.com/@LongTwentiethCentury/why-are-there-so-many-military-bases-in-djibouti-f8c579e961d5

Smith, J. M. (2017). The Mongols and The Silk Road. *The Silk Road*. Retrieved July 12, 2021, from http://www.silkroadfoundation.org/newsletter/volumeonenumberone/mongols.html

Soni, S. (2016, Feb). India-Mongolia relations in historico-cultural and contemporary perspectives. Canberra: Australian National University. Retrieved Aug 15, 2021, from https://mongoliainstitute.anu.edu.au/news-events/events/344/india-mongolia-relations-historico-cultural-and-contemporary-perspectives

Thillaikumar, D. (2018, July 27). The Mongols: Resurrection of the Silk Road, Precursors to Modern Trade. *Brewminate*. Retrieved July 12, 2021, from https://brewminate.com/the-mongols-resurrection-of-the-silk-road-precursors-to-modern-trade/

World Bank. (2006). *Mongolia's Natural Resources: A Blessing or a Curse?* The World Bank Group. Retrieved Aug 14, 2021, from https://www.worldbank.org/en/news/feature/2006/02/28/mongolias-natural-resources-blessing-or-curse

Zeidan, A. (2020, Aug). Decline of Mongol power in China. *Encyclopadia Britannica*. Retrieved Aug 15, 2021, from https://www.britannica.com/place/Mongol-empire/The-Yuan-dynasty-in-China-1279-1368#ref341059

4. The United States and Mongolia Relations: The Underrated Partnership

Sanchana Srivastava[1]

Abstract

The United States has, in recent years, touted the accomplishment of Mongolian democracy as a positive example to other nations in the region. The shift from Socialism to democracy on the part of the Mongolians has dominated both academic discourse and political speeches alike on the growing friendship between these two countries. This article argues, however, that the growing relationship between the United States and Mongolia is one based on practical benefits to both parties instead of the ideals of liberal democracy. Hence, US-Mongolia relations are based in realpolitik, not ideology. Stronger US-Mongolia relations are, and should be, based on the practical benefits each will gain from the partnership. Mongolia's benefits encompass the preservation of national independence, regional and global security, and increased domestic economic growth and infrastructure. For the US, the benefits concern Mongolia's strategic geopolitical position between Russia and China and its implications for US strategy in the region, Mongolia's access to North Korea, and finding a friend in hostile territory in the US-led war on international terrorism.

Keywords: United States, Underrated partnership, Mongolia, Realpolitik, Democracy

Introduction

The political mob of 1 July 2008 distinctly delineated that liberal majority rule system in Mongolia actually stays unsteady. Nonetheless, the US has over and over piled acclaim upon Mongolia's creating majority rule government and has

1 Sanchana Srivasatava is pursuing her Masters in International Relations at Central University of Jharkhand, Ranchi, India

"remunerated" Mongolia with more grounded political and financial relations. Much consideration has so far been given to the examination of expanded US - Mongolia relations with regards to building vote based systems in the Upper east and local Asian districts, as Mongolia advantageously falls under both geographic regions. In any case, an examination dependent on the spreading philosophy of the majority rules system as a main impetus of the expanding cooperation among Mongolia and the US is lacking, essentially because of the simple reality that Mongolia doesn't have a working liberal popular government right now. Defilement is as yet wild all through Mongolian common society, which thus stifles regular citizen interest in government and society overall. Laws drafted in accordance with vote based changes, albeit a difference from Mongolia's communist period, are not what numerous in the US consider viable with majority rules system. The legal executive remaining parts got up to speed in political defilement and its viability is as yet under question. This was crucially obvious after the 2008 mobs in which many "political dissenters" were held for quite a long time without legal executive activity. The Mongolian economy is as yet immature and defilement torment the two biggest enterprises of banking and mining, just as the traditions framework. More grounded US-Mongolia relations are, and ought to be, founded on the pragmatic benefits each will acquire from the association. Mongolia's advantages incorporate the safeguarding of public freedom, local and worldwide security, and expanded homegrown financial development and framework. For the US, the advantages concern Mongolia's key international situation among Russia and China and its suggestions for US system in the locale, Mongolia's admittance to North Korea, and finding a companion in an unfriendly area in the US-drove battle on worldwide illegal intimidation. Mongolia's choice to democratize itself following the fall of the Soviet Association has little to do with the improvement of US-Mongolia relations in the course of the last decade and a half. As referenced before, fusing the US into the North Asian provincial international system was engaged as far back as 1919, under the tyrant religious government of Bogd Khan. It very well may be contended that the fall of the Soviet Association in 1992 was simply the equivalent "reset" button that was pushed toward the finish of the Qing tradition in 1911, which left Mongolia in political limbo.

Historical analysis of U.S.-Mongolia Relations

The United States established diplomatic relations with Mongolia in 1987, and Mongolian leaders describe the United States as Mongolia's most important "third neighbor"—countries that do not border Mongolia but have close relations with it. Polling indicates Mongolian perceptions of the United States are largely positive. Mongolia's relations with its former patron Russia remain close, and many Mongolians regard Russia with some affection. At the same time, they remain wary of China, their largest economic partner. Mongolia's official relations with China largely have been amicable, with the exception of periods of tension and pressure from Beijing following visits to Mongolia, a traditionally Tibetan Buddhist country, by the Dalai Lama, the exiled Tibetan spiritual leader whom the PRC government asserts aims to split Tibet from China

Mongolia's Interest

The desire for Mongolia to improve relations between it and the US revolve around three key components: political independence, regional and global security, and economic growth.

Political independence

First and foremost, Mongolia views its growing relations with the United States as confirmation of its status as an equal member of the international community. Considering Mongolia's history of Chinese rule and Russian the most critical element in Mongolia-United States is the belief of Mongolia's "1/3 neighbor" overseas coverage. As each Russia and China have tussled over Mongol territory for over 4 hundred years, with each exercise brilliant influence (if now no longer direct rule) over it at distinctive times, another "neighbor" or out of doors energy is visible as crucial in balancing the have an impact on of each Russia and China and preserving Mongolian independence. Although the "1/3 neighbor" coverage is basically open to all international locations who desire to broaden family members with Mongolia, the Mongolian authorities perspectives relationship the United States as its essential priority. The overarching topic that dominates US-Mongolia family members is really keeping Mongolian independence. The US is engaged on this thru numerous means, the primary of that is placing itself into the conventional north Asian association of Russia-China-Mongolia family members. In line with each Mongolia's desires and US self-interest, the United States-Mongolia partnership has improved the country wide members on this framework from 3 to 4. It is the desire of Mongolia that this in flip will regulate the dynamics of the location, in order that Mongolia will circulate from being certain through Russia-China geopolitics to turning into a completely impartial member of the location and worldwide society. This may be completed specifically through diplomatic avenues.

Regional participation

In line with the above assumption, Mongolia views US involvement in Northeast Asia as essential to its participation in regional community building into which Mongolia has invested much of its foreign policy efforts. To put it bluntly, Mongolia has been, and remains, as an afterthought in these negotiations due to its perceived insignificance regarding what it can offer the region politically and economically. Although Mongolia's inclusion in any type of formal, comprehensive region-wide community building is not in question, Mongolia would like to play a larger role in these negotiations in order to solidify its position as an independent, equal nation-state. Subsequently Mongolia hopes to be incorporated into these negotiations by ensuring US support for its inclusion into any talks that may arise.

US military support

The buildup of Mongolia's military is without a doubt based on maintaining its independence. In the past Mongolia's military has been developed and maintained largely by either Soviet Russia or China. Mongolia does not wish to repeat this scenario for fear of over-reliance on its powerful neighbors, and their possible political and military coercion; so it looks to the US for support in developing Mongolia's military. As Mongolia does not share a border with the US, and has no history of US interference, it can comfortably develop a bilateral alliance with this geographically distant super power. The fear of a Chinese invasion from the south to absorb the Mongol territory previously under Chinese rule, however, has decreased dramatically since the mid to late 1980's. Nonetheless, this suspicion still lingers, given that China's growth is disproportionately high compared with other nations of the region, especially compared to Russia; and suspicion of the Chinese is an enduring theme among Mongolia's politicians and citizenry. Of greater importance to Mongolia at this time is the support of the US in building and training the Mongolian military to participate in international peace-keeping operations. Mongolia views contributing to peace-keeping forces as "a foot in the door" towards greater international participation, and thus far has contributed over 700 troops to the US-led operations in Afghanistan and Iraq. In return, the Mongolian military has benefited a great deal from US human resources, as well as monetary and technical support. The US has afforded Mongolian officers, citizens, and Foreign Service personnel the opportunity to attend military academic and training institutions across the US; engage in multiple training programs alongside US military personnel; and be given large amounts of technical support and upgrades. Moreover, as Mongolia is geographically situated at the intersection of East and Central Asia, the threat of international terrorism impacting Mongolia is real. Mongolia's western populations are made up of Muslim Kazaks whose ethnic and religious affiliations transcend Mongolia's borders. A well-equipped Mongolian military is seen as essential to address possible insecurities that may arise in Mongolia's western areas. As Mongolia and China share this common threat of growing Muslim extremism in their western territories, a competent

Mongolian military able to handle the threat of terrorism may help redress the balance in Mongolia-China relations.

Economic independence

It is seen by many in Mongolia that economic independence promotes political independence. The assistance of a major economic power besides Russia and China is essential in achieving this independence. Mongol history witnessed Qing China impose Mongolian obedience through monetary support, as well as the accumulation of massive debt on the part of Mongolian tribal leaders and the Buddhist theocracy in the eighteenth and nineteenth centuries. In contrast, the Soviet Union bankrolled virtually 80 percent of the Mongolian economy during the 70 years of Soviet influence over Mongolia in the twentieth century. As the urban populations of Mongolia increase their standard of living, Mongolian domestic politics are under more pressure to liberalize the economy. Mongolia today is the only World Trade Organization member nation that does not have a bilateral Free Trade Agreement (FTA) with any other nation. This is set to change with Mongolia's current strategy of forming an FTA with the US. Currently the US considers an FTA with Mongolia as unjustifiable on economic grounds alone, although the US is not ruling it out completely. Finally, where many of the former Soviet republics, such as the Ukraine, Georgia, Azerbaijan, and Armenia, have fostered closer ties with the European Union (culminating in the "Eastern Partnership"), Mongolia, although seeking to democratize, has no such convenient body to turn to. Considering the international clout of the US, the Mongolian government recognizes the importance of closer economic US ties in its pursuit of a more independent and economically stable Mongolia.

The United States' Interest

This section argues that the primary goal of the US in engaging Mongolia lies in Mongolia's unique position in the region and its possible benefits to US strategic interests. Mongolia's strategic geographical position.

Mongolia's strategic geographical position

The US views a strong relationship with Mongolia as beneficial to its overall Asia strategic plan, especially due to Mongolia's geographical position between Russia and China. From the end of World War II until the fall of the Soviet Union in 1992, the US's Asia strategy was based on an alliance system, often referred to as the "hub-and-spoke" model. This arrangement was essentially made up of a few strategically important allies that entered into bilateral defense relationships with the US. This has, for the most part, kept conflict in the region subdued in comparison to the era before World War II. The Chinese government generally saw US troops based in Japan as beneficial, as a large US military presence in Japan prevented a re-occurrence of imperial ambitions by the Japanese on the Asian continent. A US presence in Asia allowed China to undertake economic reforms to modernize with no real military threat, and South Korea viewed US troops on its side of the Demilitarized Zone as necessary for peace on the Korean Peninsula. However, although US soldiers did not leave either Japan or South Korea, the US strategy in Asia following the Cold War shifted from a dominant focus on security to a mixture of security and economic issues. This was evident during the Clinton Administration's China policy, where it chose to engage China economically instead of containing or countering its rapid rise either regionally or globally. Since that time, China has argued that its rise is peaceful and has, to the surprise of many, embraced multilateralism as a core foreign policy. However, China still asserts its sovereignty over ethnic minority areas such as Tibet, Xinjiang (the Muslim Uighur population), and Inner Mongolia. The ethnic unrest seen in Tibet has not been contained and Xinjiang has also recently developed into an ethnic/religious hotspot within China's borders. This unrest could possibly spill over into Inner Mongolia as well. Islamic fundamentalism is already a real concern in Xinjiang, and even though pan-Mongolianism is subdued, it is still present in Inner Mongolia. One significant factor in China's rise is whether China can contain these ethnic "domestic" issues. Given their ethnic nature, these domestic issues could put China's economic growth in the region on a collision course with the national interests of some or all of its Central Asian neighbors, given that these ethnic issues inevitably transcend modern nation-state borders. As US interests are embedded in the Central Asian region, where the fi the former Soviet countries of Kazakhstan, Kyrgyzstan, Turkmenistan, Tajikistan, and Uzbekistan have been instrumental in the US-led "War on Terror" in Afghanistan and Iraq, conflict between the US and China is not out of the question. If China is coerced to change the status quo of the Central Asian region and engage with it more forcefully due to domestic issues spilling over China's borders, US interests in the region will inevitably be at risk. A conflict of interest is likely between China and the US over large deposits of oil, natural gas, uranium, and gold. As these resources are located in the Central Asia region, the US views Mongolia as a convenient ally in its relations with China. A US-Mongolia military partnership could relieve unnecessary pressure if a conflict of interest between the US and China arose in Central Asia. Mongolia's location at the intersection of Northeast and Central Asia could provide a diffusing mechanism for the US military in the event of a possible confrontation with China. Furthermore, a US presence in Mongolia would ensure US influence in the region by in effect coercing China, North Korea, and Russia to include the US in any regional security or economic dialogue. The US already has a firm foothold in the region with military bases in Japan and South Korea. However, Mongolia's efforts to establish closer US relations is incredibly convenient, as it pushes the US presence further to the north and northwest, inserting itself in what has traditionally been a solid block of exclusively Russian and Chinese negotiated territory. As with US-China relations, US-Russia relations in Central Asia highlight for the US the significance of an alliance with Mongolia. In early February 2009, Kyrgyzstan announced its plans to close a strategic US air base that has been critical to US missions into Afghanistan. Many observers see this as a decision influenced by Russia to squeeze the US out of Central Asia. Upon the announcement by Kyrgyzstan, Russia immediately offered its support for the US to use Russian bases for its Afghan operations, a move which would place US actions in Central Asia under tighter scrutiny from Russia's watchful eye. Although the US negotiated with the Kyrgyzstan government effectively and avoided this roadblock, the US will need to give up increasingly more negotiating power to ensure its place in the region. As Russia once again exerts itself internationally, moves like this cause the US to seek other options. Mongolia, with one foot in Central Asia and the other foot outside the region, provides an opportune alternative. Although Russia views Mongolia directly within its sphere of influence, as it does the former Soviet Central Asian nations, Russia's grip on Mongolia has softened since Gorbachev's Valdiviostock speech in 1986 and the subsequent fall of the Soviet Union in 1992. Since that time, Mongolia's position between the Soviet Union and China was vital in rebuilding Russia, as Russia held on to virtually all of Siberia. Due to a diminished threat from China, coupled with the domestic push by Mongolia to distance itself from Russia, Russia has backed away from Mongolia considerably since then. For the US, Mongolia's decision to seek a "third neighbor" is strategically in line with US foreign policy interests.

North Korea relations

The North Korean nuclear issue is of vital concern to the US in the Northeast Asian region. Maintaining the status quo that emerged after the Korean War is vital to maintaining a US presence in the region. Although Mongolia's declaration of itself as a "Nuclear Free Territorial Zone" was initially intended as a reaction to its position between the two nuclear powers of Russia and China and its experience during the Sino-Soviet conflict, it does hold positive implications for the US in its mediation with North Korea. As Endicott (2005: 23) says:

> I regret that we have not been able to witness a 7-Party Talks in Beijing where Mongolia could play a significant facilitator role in its ongoing quest to help improve the security of the region.

Mongolia has also been instrumental in "Track II" negotiations In July 1986, Soviet Head of State Gorbachev gave a speech in Vladivostok outlining the Soviet Union's new Asia policy and positive re-engagement with China. This had implications on Mongolia's relations with both China and the West, as China had established relations with the United States in 1979.

Combating international terrorism

The US views Mongolia as a key player in its fight against the spread of international terrorism. To date, Mongolia has contributed over 700 of its military personnel to the US-led operations in Afghanistan and Iraq. The ratio of servicemen who served in Iraq and Afghanistan to Mongolia's total population (which is roughly 2.7 million) ranks Mongolia's contribution to the wars in Afghanistan and Iraq higher than those of Japan and South Korea; both of which are established allies of the US. Mongolia's strategic location gives closer access to potential terrorist "hot spots," such as Central Asia and Northwestern China (Xinjiang). A stable and independent Mongolia is of the utmost importance to the US, whether it is a democracy or an authoritarian theocracy, as it was at the start of the twentieth century. What is our important to the US is that Mongolia gains and maintains its political distance

Conclusion

The mutual interest of both the countries have been emphasized upon different aspects. On January 27, 2017, Mongolia and the United States celebrated the 30th anniversary of their diplomatic relations at the Embassy of Mongolia in Washington DC. While the two countries have gone through different phases of development, reform, and economic booms and crises in their domestic environments, the achievements in their bilateral ties were rooted in shared principles and values. During the past 30 years, Mongolia and the United States have augmented relations through diplomatic means in the political, economic, social, and military spheres. Mongolia made a few attempts to engage the United States even while still under the heavy influence of Russia and China. Boosting ties with Mongolia could be a way for the US to show China it has found an alternative country that can meet its rare-earth demands. This would reduce US reliance on China in this regard.

References

Auslin, Michael. 2008. "A Third Neighbor Strategy for Asia," Asian Outlook. American Enterprise Institute for Public Policy Research (3 October), [online] http://www.aei.org/outlook/28731 (accessed on 13 December 2008).

Batbayar, Ts. 2006. "Mongolia's Post-Soviet Identity and New External Environment." Mongolica, An International Annual of Mongol Studies, 17(38): 187-195.

Batbayar, Tsedendamba. 2003. "Foreign Policy and Domestic Reform in Mongolia." Central Asian Survey 22.1 (March): 45-59.

Batbayar, Tsedendambyn. 1999. "Mongolian Perspectives on Northeast Asian Regional Development."Pp 207-223 in Politics and Economics in Northeast Asia: Nationalism and Regionalism in Contention. Bloomsburg: MacMillan Press.

Batchimeg, Migeddorg. 2005. "Mongolia-China Relations and its Implications on Mongolia-US Relations." Pp 46-58 in A Comprehensive US-Mongolia Partnership: Challenges and Opportunities. Regional Security Issues and Mongolia, The Institute for Strategic Studies, Vol. XXVI/MMIV. Proceedings of the Bilateral Conference (28 February – 1 March 2005).

Campi, Alicia Jean. 1987. The Political Relationship between the United States and Outer Mongolia, 1915-1927: Kalgan Consular Records. Bloomington: Indiana University.

Endicott, Dr. John E. 2005. "Mongolia-US Comprehensive Relationship." Pp 18-30 in A Comprehensive US-Mongolia Partnership: Challenges and Opportunities. Regional Security Issues and Mongolia, The Institute for Strategic Studies, Vol. XXVI/MMIV. Proceedings of the Bilateral Conference (28 February – 1 March 2005).

Gilberg, Rolf and Jan-Olof Svantesson. 1996. "The Mongols, Their Land and History," in Mongolia in Transition: Old Patterns, New Challenges, Ole Bruun and Ole Odgaard (eds), Nordic Institute of Asian Studies. Great Britain: Curzon Press.

Gombo, Enebish. 2007. Interviewed by Ron Porter, 4 August. Green, Elizabeth E. 1986. "China and Mongolia: Recurring Trends and Prospects for Change," Asian Survey 26.12 (December): 1337-1363.

Janhunen, Juha. 2006. "Mongolia and China: Geopolitical Implications of the Unequal Relationship," in Mongolica, An International Annual of Mongol Studies, Vol. 17 (38): 213-219.

Kennedy, William. 2008. "After Six Weeks, Mongolian Lawmaker, Demonstrator Posts Bail." [online] http://ubpost.mongolnews.mn/index.php?option=com_content&task=view&id=2139&Itemid=37 The UB Post Online [Ulaanbaatar], 14 August (accessed on 26 January 2009).

Khirghis, Munkh-Ochir, D. 2005. "Mongolia-US Comprehensive Partnership: Opportunities and Challenges." Pp 31-45 in A Comprehensive US-Mongolia Partnership: Challenges and Opportunities, Regional Security Issues and Mongolia. The Institute for Strategic Studies, Vol. XXVI/MMIV. Proceedings of the Bilateral Conference (28 February – 1 March).

La Porta, Ambassador Alphonse F. 2005. "Free Trade Agreement between Mongolia and US: Illusion or Reality? (The US View)." Pp 60-65 in A Comprehensive US-Mongolia Partnership: Challenges and Opportunities. Regional Security Issues and Mongolia, The Institute for Strategic Studies, Vol. XXVI/MMIV. Proceedings of the Bilateral Conference (28 February – 1 March 2005).

5. Indo-Mongolian Relations in Present Era

Dr. Mukesh H. Khatik and Ms. Upasana Bhandari[1]

Abstract

At present, there is a good a synergy between Mongolia and India .both country has emerged as a good neighbouring country past to present and they respect each other as part of their foreign policy. Mongolia focuses today on a number of pressing domestic socio-economic issues. Unemployment, poverty, rapid urbanization and the ensuing social displacement pose potential threats to long-term stability and economic prosperity. Moreover, it becomes a more difficult task in the absence of a meaningful regional cooperation framework. India's new role in East Asia may have far-reaching consequences to the extent of benefiting Mongolia as well so far as issue of regional cooperation is concerned. Mongolia could seek India's support and recent developments in India-Mongolia ties make it more feasible. India, as a close friend and considered by Mongolia as its spiritual neighbour, would like to see Mongolia flourish and prosper in building and strengthening democratic traditions and institutions, apart from its economic and developmental achievements. Ever since Mongolia become independent till now 2021, they have been cooperate each other in all issue of bilateral and multilateral but another thing it does not mean that Mongolia does not have relation with other countries they have because of its geo-political condition and its own national interest. Most important thing relation with India both bind up with Buddhism, historically and culturally and they continued to build relation based on.

Keywords: Cultural, Historical, Economic, Security council, Defence, Cyber Security, Military, Foreign policy, Trade, Terrorism, Civilization, Bilateral, Treaty, Defence, Democracy, Global Peace.

---

1 Dr. Mukesh H. Khatik is Assistant Professor and Head Dept. of Political Science, USSS, Gujarat University, Ahmedabad and Ms. Upasana Bhandari is an independent researcher.

Introduction

India and Mongolia relation is more than 2750 years old historical and culturally based and it is in a good shape India's position as a third neighbour give a defined direction to Mongolia foreign policy. Traditionally Mongolia has never been neglected in India. Currently India's relations with Mongolia are getting wider but we cannot say that India is taking interest in Mongolia because of China ,it has always been India's maintain its political freedom of Mongolia as it was an earlier under the influence of the Soviet Union now it should not come completely under the influence of China. However, one most must not forget that democracy and Buddhism are the key element that bind India with Mongolia in addition to successful diplomacy being pursued by the two sides towards each other after Modi took over power in 2014 India's foreign policy has taken new direction not only towards neighbours but also towards these extended neighbourhood. As regards East Asia since 1993 India's look east policy had been working well until Modi government took a resolute stand to make India's vigorous presence in the region the result was that look east policy was change into active policy with this new policy Northeast Asia also comes into promises in India's foreign policy. Mongolia which belongs to the Northeast Asia became a key country in India active policy while India became a key third neighbour country in Mongolia's foreign policy. It is also true that China has replaced the Soviet Union in Mongolia no one country can replace China in Mongolia because has made a lot of economic promotion trade and investment in Mongolia, but Mongolian public might be impressed by their excessive economic offers. Foreign Policy: Mongolia seeks to attain its foreign policy goals in a "multi-pillared" global environment. Sovereignty, national pride, national security, territorial integrity is the cornerstones of Mongolia's foreign policy. Mongolia has diplomatic relations with 140 countries in the world. Having for long lived in an external environment, which was dominated by the geographic fact of Russian and Chinese presence on its borders, Mongolia, since the decades of 90s, after complete independence and adoption of free market economic policies has pursued an independent foreign policy. Mongolia has sought to build bridges with other global players through the doctrine of "third neighbour" which includes USA, Japan, India, ROK and EU. Due to deep and ancient Buddhist links through Tibet, India is also referred to as the "spiritual neighbour" of Mongolia. Mongolia has pursued the policy of joining hands with international initiatives and multinational fora.

Over the year India relationship with Mongolia has been widening to include strategic element such as the uranium from Mongolia. Defence Corporation has grown and the militaries of the two countries conduct exercise "NOMAD ELEPHANT" regularly. There is also mutual consultation on between the security council of the two countries on topic like cyber securities have been given importance Mongolia strategic position at the cross junction of Central Asia Northeast Asia east West and China Russia attract major power towards. For the United States Mongolia is an important partner in its PIVOT to Asia. India should consider Mongolia as the Green Zone economic development that absorbs high tech features and production skills in a modernization process to preserve and promotional common heritage of Indo Mongolian culture is important this should serve as the basis for nurturing and pursuing future common interest there is a regular consultation between the National Security Council of India and Mongolia on issue of mutual interest in regional multilateral affairs including on the subject of terrorism in recent years Modi visit to Mongolia the renewal of defence cooperation agreement is considered to a very important as it may give a boost to India's foreign policy of engaging with the neighbours of China in a move discreet manner. There is no doubt India and Mongolia in their history and culture have created a background for political economic and defines religion in the contemporary period. That in recent years especially after Modi visit to Mongolia the strategic partnership between the two countries has been giving a boost to enhancing their bilateral relationship which has further been strengthened with the visit of the Mongolian president Battulga that to India. This only confirms that both sides give the importance to each other in their respective foreign policy.

Mythological Perspective

India and Mongolia have interacted through the medium of Buddhism over a period 2700 years this process of cultural and spiritual interaction has enriched the two civilizations through the process of give and take. The two countries continued to build relation based on shared historical cultural legacy.

Diplomatic Relations with Mongolia

Diplomatic relation between India and Mongolia were established on 24 December 1955 .India was the first country outside the soviet block to establish diplomatic relation with Mongolia India's role in security UN member for is acknowledged by the Mongolian people, Mongolia also appreciation for India's support for its admission to non-aligned movement (NAM) as a full member in 1991. Year 2020 marked the 65th anniversary of establishment of diplomatic relations. In January 1956, we had first Mongolian Ambassador in New Delhi. Indian resident Mission in Ulaanbaatar was opened on 22 February 1971. Earlier, Indian Ambassador in Moscow (T.N. Kaul) was concurrently accredited. Mongolians appreciate Indian's support to its membership in United Nations in 1961 which was championed by Pt. Jawaharlal Nehru. In 1991, India supported Mongolia's membership to Non-

Aligned Movement (NAM). Mongolia along with India and Bhutan co-sponsored famous Resolution for the recognition of Bangladesh as an independent country in 1972

Treaty of Friendly Relation: Joint declaration of 1973 & Cooperation of 1994

According these treaty- both country developing equally and mutually beneficial co-operation in various spheres including political, economic, trade, science, technology, health, agriculture, ecology, culture, education, communication and terrorism.

Development of links between two parliament's government and NGO on both sides Co-operation, bilateral and multi-lateral, combating international crime including terrorism, cyber security. Mongolia and India have been cooperating with each other in the area of cyber security domain. Mongolian Prime Minister expressed his appreciation to India's support to set up a cyber-security centre in Mongolia. Economic Cooperation closely cooperation with in the frame work of the UN, NAM, and other international organization with a view to furthering the cause of peace and international security, globally and in Asia, India and Mongolia support the evolution of open, balanced and inclusive security architecture in the Asia Pacific region based on collective efforts, considering legitimate interests of all states of the region guided by respect for norms and principles of international law. The two Prime Ministers reiterated their readiness to strengthen regional as well as multilateral cooperation, including through enhanced interaction in the UN and other regional and international organizations.

Some important visit of two countries India and Mongolia: The first ever and historic visit of Prime Minister Shri Narendra Modi to Mongolia (16-18 May 2015) as a part of 'Act East' policy, has proven to be a watershed period for India Mongolia relations. The declaration of 'Strategic Partnership', signing of 22-pointJoint Statement, announcement of USD 1 Billion LoC for development of Infrastructure in Mongolia – now being utilized for building 1st Oil Refinery - and 13 agreements prime minister Shri Narendra Modi visit Mongolia in May 2015 to mark the 60th anniversary of establishment of diplomatic relation between India and Mongolia brought in a paradigm shift in our relationship .the monument this generated has been sustained by several high level exchange in last four year two Prime Ministers underscored the significance of the visit in the backdrop of the 60th anniversary of diplomatic relations between Mongolia and India. It is the first ever visit by an Indian Prime Minister marking the dawn of a new era in Mongolia-India relations paved the way for elevation of our partnership to 'Strategic' level. 13 G2G agreements and 4 B2B agreements signed to expand our economic cooperation in various areas have come to manifest India's image as a strong 'third neighbour' has taken strong roots in the minds of Mongolian public and government structure. India's gifting of 150,000 doses of Covid Vaccine on Feb 22, 2021 was billed as a "historic" moment by Mongolian Deputy Prime Minister, as it was the Mongolia's first vaccine came from India.

They further noted with satisfaction the continued development of bilateral relations in the framework of a comprehensive partnership based on deep civilizational, historical, spiritual and cultural linkages, common democratic traditions and shared desire for regional as well as international peace and stability.

Given the shared desire to remain trusted partners, the two Prime Ministers pledged to further consolidate India-Mongolia comprehensive partnership, and agreed to elevate the level of the comprehensive partnership to a Strategic Partnership that is conducive to the common cause of the international community for peace and prosperity, and aligned with the collective interests of our two countries and our peoples.

Political and Security Partnership

The two Prime Ministers noted with satisfaction the increased high-level exchanges between the two countries in recent years and how these exchanges have significantly reinforced the momentum for cooperation between the two countries. Acknowledging the importance to maintain the frequency of reciprocal visits, both Prime Ministers noted that the nature and spread of international terrorism in recent years poses a threat to all humanity and requires global resolve and cooperative measures of the international community without double standards or selectivity. They agreed to direct concerned officials to work together for the adoption of the comprehensive convention on international terrorism. The Prime Ministers expressed hope that all safe havens and sanctuaries for terrorists will be wiped out without delay. Further, they also agreed to promote the exchanges of visits at all levels, namely between the government leaders, ministers, parliamentarians and senior officials and regular political dialogue on the side lines of multilateral events.

Bilateral Defence and Security Cooperation

The two Prime Ministers agreed to continue to work towards further intensifying bilateral defence and security cooperation through exchanges of high and mid-level visits, regular consultations and dialogue between the ministries of defence and other relevant organizations, including the national security councils, military personnel exchanges, capacity building, technical cooperation, special a Joint Working Group for Defence cooperation also convened annually. Mr. N. Enkhbold,

Minister of Defence visited India in March 2018 and held bilateral talks with RRM, RM, NSA and COAS. The 8th JWG met in New Delhi (13-14 December 2016) and the Mongolian delegation was led by Deputy Defence Minister. The 9th JWG held from 6-8 May 2019 in Ulaanbaatar headed by JS (Air) and Mongolian Deputy Minister of Defence. zed vocational training, joint exercises in Special Forces and information security, collaboration in UN as well as to other international peacekeeping operations. Joint India-Mongolia exercise 'Nomadic Elephant' is held annually. Last year it was held at Ulaanbaatar (Mongolia) from 10-22 September 2018 and in 2019 it was held from 05-18 October 2019 at Bakloh (HP), India. During 2020, it could not be held due to Covid enforced environment and is now expected to be held in the last quarter of 2021.Indian Armed Forces Observers regularly participate in the Annual multilateral peacekeeping exercise 'Khan Quest' in Mongolia. For 2021 exercises scheduled to be held in July.

Commercial, Economic and Technical Cooperation

The two Prime Ministers agreed to encourage development of equal and mutually beneficial trade, investment and economic cooperation, which is balanced, sustainable, and leads to prosperity in both countries. India and Mongolia signed MoU for establishment for joint trade, subcommittee and cooperation between the planning commission of India national development board of Mongolia were signed in 1994 to expand bilateral economic trade and agreement on trade and economic cooperation for MFN status to each other customs duties all other taxes on import and export, geology and mineral resources entered in September 1996. The mission regularly contributes consolidating and strengthening our trade and bilateral relation especially highlighted that Mongolia is beneficiary of India's single largest LoC for construction in December 2018, the embassy in coloration with Mongolia national chamber of commerce and industry organised commercial event, trade and investment opportunities in India to promote Indian pharmaceutical, agriculture, dairy, spice, tea, coffee, tourism and education sector in Mongolia.

Holding of two important Buddhist international conferences – Asian Buddhist Conference on Peace (ABCP) and Samvaad-III Buddhism-Hinduism Global Dialogue in Gandan Monastery in May and Sept 2019 respectively - in which India plays an important role, have contributed to consolidating of this shared heritage in recent years. As a part of 65th diplomatic anniversary celebrations, in April 2020, our Ministry of Culture have started reprinting of about 100 sets of '108 volumes of Mongolian Kanjur', which is expected to be completed in 2022. Incidentally, 25 volume set was virtually handed over by EAM to the then Chief Cabinet Secretary Mr Oyun Erdene (now Prime Minister) during the 7th Joint Commission Meeting. Subsequently, Prime Minister Shri Narendra Modi with Prime Minister J. Erdenebat met in the side lines of St. Petersburg International Economic Forum (June2017) and also met thrice with the current President Kh Battulga on the margins of Shanghai Cooperation Organization Summit at Qingdao, China (June 2018) and Eastern Economic Forum (EEF) in Vladivostok (Sep 2019) before holding full bilateral meeting in New Delhi during his State Visit to India (Sept 2019). PMs Meeting with Mongolian President was prominently noted in Mongolian media for enhancing bilateral relations.

Bilateral Cooperation Mechanism: India and Mongolia have 'India-Mongolia Joint Committee on Cooperation (IMJCC)' chaired at Ministerial level. 5th meeting of IMJCC was held in New Delhi in April, 2016 under the Chair of MoS for EA Gen (Retd.) V.K. Singh and Mr. L. Purevsuren, Foreign Minister of Mongolia. The 6th meeting of IMJCC was held in Ulaanbaatar on 25 April, 2018 co-chaired by Smt. Sushma Swaraj, External Affairs Minister and Mr. D. Tsogtbaatar, Foreign Minister of Mongolia. Owingto scheduling difficulties, the 7th IMJCC was not held in 2019 and finally took place virtually due to Covid enforced environment on Dec 3, 2020 and co-chairmanship of Dr. S. Jaishankar, External Affairs Minister and Mr. L. Oyun-Erdene, the then Chief Cabinet Secretary (Prime Minister since Jan 27, 2021).

Foreign Office Consultations

The last round of FOCs was held on 23 December 2016 in Ulaanbaatar. JS (EA) in MEA led the Indian side. The Acting Director, Department of Asia, Africa & Pacific Regions co-chaired the consultations from the Mongolian side. Though the Mongolian State Secretary of MFA visited India in the first week of November 2018 & held bilateral issues, it was not considered as FOC. The next round of FOCs is expected to be held in New Delhi at Secretary Level depending on mutually convenient dates. Co-operation in UN & International Organizations: Mongolia has been traditionally supporting India and Indian candidates in the United Nations and various other international forums. It has supported us for the non-permanent seat of the UN Security Council (UNSC) for 2011-2012. India and Mongolia agreed to support to each other for UNSC non-permanent seats respectively for terms 2021-22 and2023-24. Mongolia voted in favour of India's proposal to Yoga's inscription into the list of UNESCO's Intangible Cultural Heritage. India also voted for registering Mongolian legacy on "Mongolian Traditional Custom to Worship Mountain and Ovoo" in the list of Intangible Cultural Heritage. Mongolia has publicly reiterated its support for India's membership to the permanent seat of expanded UNSC. Since 2017, Mongolian supported Indian candidature to:

- International Tribunal for the Law of the Sea (ITLOS)
- Executive Board of UNESCO for the term 2017-2021
- World Custom Organization (WCO)

- Council of the International Maritime Organization (IMO) in Category 'B' during the 30th session of the IMO Assembly in 2017,
- Advisory Committee membership election for Human Rights Council during the 36th meeting of HRC in Geneva in 2017
- International Court of Justice [For ICJ Mongolia's support was on reciprocal basis]
- Executive Board of the UNESCO at 39th General Conference for term 2017-2021
- 3rd group of International Civil Aviation Organization (ICAO) during the 40th Assembly, 2019
- World Anti-Doping Agency (WADA) for the term 2020-2022
- Council of the International Maritime Organization (IMO) in Category 'B' during the 31st session of the IMO Assembly in 2019
- World Custom Organisation (xi) World Custom Organization (WCO)
- Asia Pacific Group seat of the UN Security Council for the term 2021-22
- Inter-governmental Committee for the Safeguard of Intangible Cultural Heritage
- UN Advisory Committee on Administrative and Budgetary (ACABQ) in November 2020

Border Patrolling Cooperation

The BSF (MHA) of India and the Mongolian General Authority for Border Protection (GABP) has been closely cooperating on border patrolling and related subjects for over eight years. Several proposals on capacity building& technical assistance, including supply of integrated server to GABP by BSF are under consideration and likely to be completed by mid-2021provided COVID-19 situation in both countries is eased.

Disaster Management Cooperation

National Emergency Management Agency (NEMA) and National Disaster Management Agency (NDMA) picked up pace in the recent years. In 2018, 25 officers of NEMA were trained in India under ITEC. During the visit of President of Mongolia to India in September, 2019, a MoU on cooperation in the field of Disaster Management and Disaster Risk Reduction was signed between NEMA of Mongolia and NDMA of India and an 'Action Plan' for2021-2022 has also been negotiated between the two agencies in Feb 2021. However, some of the proposed activities in 2020-2021 could not be held due to Covid pandemic.

Energy Cooperation

A Working Group for cooperation in the field of nuclear energy has been set up between the respective agencies of the two countries i.e. the DAE and the Nuclear Energy Agency of Mongolia.

Mongolia like rest of the world was impacted badly during 2020 owing to Covid pandemic.

126

However, using technological tools, the mission still organized 6-virtual 'Webinars' dedicated to Mining & Mineral Cooperation, Healthcare and Pharma sector, Smart Cities, IT and related technologies, Dairy, Agriculture and Animal Husbandry sectors during Oct 2020 to Feb 2021 and another Virtual Meeting by Policy Times of India on 'Unleashing India's potential' was organized in Feb 2021 to bridge asymmetry of information and promote bilateral trade and commerce between India and Mongolia

Notwithstanding our excellent relations, the volume of bilateral trade is modest in value & volumes. Main items of exports to Mongolia include medicines, mining, machinery and auto parts, etc. Imports from Mongolia include raw cashmere wool. However, India-Mongolia bilateral trade has registered significant growth during the last five years (2016-2020) as evident from the tables (Table 1 & Table 2) given below:

Table 1: Bilateral Trade

Bilateral Trade Amount (in USD Million)					
Trade	**2016**	**2017**	**2018**	**2019**	**2020**
Export	2.232	1.788	0.995	1.154	0.741
Import	24.757	35.878	51.752	37.143	34.608

(Sources: MNCCI)

Table 2: Participation of Mongolian companies in commercial events during 2020-21

S. No.	Date & Month	Name Of Event	Place
1.	21 February 2020	India Soft 2020	Hyderabad
2.	24 December 2020	Online webinar (Zoom application) – on Agriculture	Mongolia
3.	05 January 2021	Online webinar (Zoom application) – on Dairy Product & Animal Husbandry	Mongolia

4.	07 January 2021	Online webinar (Zoom application) – on Smart city and roll out of COVID Vaccine	Mongolia
5.	21 January 2021	Online webinar (Zoom application) – on export of coking coal to India	Mongolia
6.	04 February 2021	Online webinar (Zoom application) – on Oil Refinery Project	Mongolia
7.	10 February 2021	Online webinar (Zoom application) – on Coal organised by Coal Preparation Society of India	New Delhi
[Due to COVID-19 pandemic, Mongolian companies could not participate in commercial events physically from March 2020 to February, 2021]			

(Sources: MNCCI)

ITEC Assistance

During Ex-President Elbegdorj's visit to India in 2009, 120slots per annum were offered to Mongolia under Indian Technical and Economic Cooperation (ITEC). From 2011-12, the number of these slots for civilian training programme were increased to 150 per year. e 2019-20, Ministry has approved 200 slots n 2020.Of the 200 allocated slots for FY 2020-21, only 2 slots were utilized for online training by NCCD, Mongolia Doctors in May, 2020 and the remaining slots have not been unutilized due to COVID-19 situation in both the countries.

Humanitarian Assistance

Worth USD 20,000 in the form of beds, bedrolls, toys, etc. for the children of herders in Sukhbaatar Aimag (severely affected by harsh winter 'Zud') was provided Mongolian experts on solar energy has been organized in India. Humanitarian assistance worth USD 50,000 was provided by the Government of India to the flood affected Provinces (Bayan Ulgii, Arhangai and Huvsgul) of Mongolia in August 2018.

Medical Missions

A team of 17 Indian Rotarians doctors led by Mr. R. K. Saboo, Ex-President of Rotary International undertook the second medical mission to Mongolia in May 2019 and conducted about 300 surgeries and donated medical equipment / medicines worth USD 12000. The first medical mission was undertaken by them in August 2017.

Digital Connectivity Network

The Government of Mongolia sought India's assistance on expansion of network in rural areas and improvement of infrastructure of main ICT network. Proposal is under consideration.

Cultural Cooperation

The India-Mongolian Agreement on Cultural Cooperation was first signed in 1961 and a CEP between the two countries has always remained in force. The Agreement envisages co-operation in the fields of education by way of scholarships, exchange of experts, participation in conferences etc. The CEP was renewed in 2003, 2005, 2009and 2015 and most recently in Sept 2019 during the visit of Mongolian President until 2022. A "Festival of India" was organized in 2015 by the mission to mark the 60 years of diplomatic relations with Mongolia was organized in November 2015. A dance troupe from Mongolia performed in various cities in India in January 2018 and a traditional Indian Dance Troupe performed in 3 cities in Mongolia including capital city Ulaanbaatar in March 2018. A special Laddakh Mask Dance troupe visited Mongolia to perform at the Asian Buddhist Conference on Peace (ABCP) in June 2019 and also performed in Darkhan Province. There are regular exchanges of cultural troupe and performances of Indian performing groups that are well appreciated in Mongolia. In 2019, the mission has set up 5 special 'India-corners' at Rajeev Gandhi Polytechnic Institute.

Atal Bihari Vajpayee Centre for Excellence in ICT

An agreement was signed in September 2001 during the visit of Minister for IT Pramod Mahajan to Mongolia, the Atal Bihari Vajpayee Centre of Excellence (ABVCE) in Information and Communication Technology (ICT) in Mongolia and 5 Community Information Centres (CICs) in 5provinces (Khovsgol, Bulgan, Kharkhorin, Darkhan - Uuland Sukhbaatar). However, subsequently, at the request of Mongolian Ministry of Education (MMoE) it was decided that instead of 5 small centres, a full-fledged Centre of Excellence would be established using LoC of USD 20 million. PM Modi along with Mongolian PM laid the foundation stone of this centre of this Centre within the campus of Mongolian University of Science and Technology (MUST) in May 2015.

Solar Energy

The first solar energy electrification project from India was executed by the Central Electronics Ltd. and formally inaugurated in April 2006 in Dadal Soum. Training of Mongolian expert on solar energy has been organized in India. Medical Missions: May 2019 and conducted about 300 surgeries and donated medical equipment / medicines worth USD 12000. The first medical mission was undertaken by them in August 2017 when Indian doctors conducted neurosurgery, microsurgery, anaesthesiology, audiology, plastic surgery, etc. a Medical equipment worth of USD 30,000/- (approximately) donated to various Mongolian hospitals. Indian Rotarian have offered to treat 10 Mongolian poor children free of cost for their heart surgeries. The offer was reportedly utilized by Mongolian children in 2018 through the India-Mongolia Health Cooperation Centre.

Conclusion

It may be said that the richness of relationship between India and Magnolia is a result of the long standing people to people contact, mutual understanding between the people of both countries through enhancing education and cultural cooperation and common demarcating tradition and shared desired for regional as well as international peace and stability. India and Magnolia comprehensive partnership and agree to elevate the level of the comprehensive partnership to the strategic partnership that is conducive common cause of the international community for peace and prosperity, aligned with collective interest of two countries and its people. India and Magnolia relationship in present era would be the common yet new objective of the respective foreign policies.

References:

Embassy of India, Ulanbatar, http://www.eoi.gov.in/ulaanbaatar/

Embassy of India, Ulaanbaatar website: http://www.eoi.gov.in/ulaanbaatar/

Embassy of India, Ulanbatar, http://www.eoi.gov.in/ulaanbaatar-Mongolia-Embassy-of-IndiaUlaanbaatar/209956815734086?ref=hl

TOI (May 17, 2015). Joint Statement for India-Mongolia Strategic Partnership, Retrieved from https://timesofindia.indiatimes.com/india/joint-statement-for-india-mongolia-strategic-partnership/articleshow/47315412.cms

Powell, E.(2006).Mongolia.Archaeology,59(1),16-23. http://www.jstor.org/stable/41781443

Sneath, D. (2011). Mapping and the Headless State: Rethinking National Populist Concepts of Mongolia. In Sabloff P. (Ed.), Mapping Mongolia: Situating Mongolia in the World from Geologic Time to the Present (pp. 34-59). University of Pennsylvania Press. http://www.jstor.org/stable/j.ctt3fhwrc.10

Frederic, Gare and Mattoo, Amitabh (Eds) (2001). India and ASEAN-The politics of India's look East Policy, Manohar Publishers, New Delhi.

Nagarajan S. (1998). Buddhism in South East Asia, Report of the Centre for Studies on Indo-China and South Pacific, Tirupati.

Oidov, Nyamdavaa (2015). Ancient Cultural, Ethnic and Religious Ties between Mongolia and India, World Affairs: The Journal of International Issues, Vol. 19, No. 4 (WINTER (OCTOBER-DECEMBER) 2015, pp. 150-159.

Hall, Ian (2012). India's New Public Diplomacy: Soft Power and the Limits of Government Action, Asian Survey 52 (6s): 1089–1110. doi:10.1525/as.2012.52.6.1089.

Sharad, Soni K (2006). India's New Role in East Asia: Implications for Mongolia, Mongolian Journal of International Affairs No.13 2006 pp.32-41. DOI: 10.5564/mjia.v0i13.6.

6. Situating Tajikistan in India's Central Asia Policy: A Strategic Dimension

Dr Pravesh Kumar Gupta[1]

Abstract

India and Tajikistan share deep historical and cultural relations. Tajikistan was a part of the Kushana and Persian Empire, which had close cultural linkages with India. Throughout the Islamic rule in India, the Persian language and Sufism from Turkestan got assimilated into Indian society. It has become the foundation of cultural and linguistic cooperation in modern times. Tajikistan's strategic location makes it significant for India's Central Asia policy. It is regarded as India's 'Gateway to Central Asia.' The Wakhan Corridor, a narrow strip in Afghanistan divides India from Tajikistan. A major challenge in enhancing bilateral ties between the two countries has been the lack of direct connectivity. Tajikistan shares a direct border with Afghanistan and has always been vulnerable to the dissemination of terrorism, extremism and drug trafficking in its territory. Similarly, India faces a direct threat from radical forces being supported and propagated by Pakistan within its territory and in Afghanistan. Therefore, India-Tajikistan cooperation in the security and defence sector has been fundamental for their economic and political relations.

In 2015, PM Modi visited five Central Asian countries in one go, including Tajikistan, which is considered a landmark in enhancing India's footprint in Central Asia. In October 2018, Indian President Sri Ramnath Kovind and a high-level delegation paid an official visit to Tajikistan and met with his Tajik counterpart; defence and security remained the key points of discussion between the two leaders. These high-level visits and discussions have strengthened the bilateral cooperation framework despite the absense of land connectivity. India is working towards bridging this gap of connectivity by investing in the development of Chabahar port in Iran and the International North-South Transport Corridor

1 Dr Pravesh Kumar Gupta is a Research Associate at Vivekananda International Foundation, New Delhi

(INSTC). India's multi-billion humanitarian and developmental assistance to Afghanistan is also intended to stabilize the country, as without a stabilize Afghanistan; India's aspirations of connecting with Central Asia could not be achieved. This paper would assess the significance of Tajikistan as an aspect of India's extended neighbourhood policy. Also, the regional factors affecting their relations will be critically examined in this research paper.

Keywords: India, Tajikistan, Central Asia, Foreign Policy, Stability, Afghanistan, INSTC, Connectivity, Iran

Introduction

India's links with Central Asia can be traced back long before the emergence of the Silk Route, which transported commodities, people, and ideas. However, a scholarly focus on the Silk Road connection has ignored the splendour of the Pre-Silk Route connection between India and Central Asia.[1] A close observation of the historical ties establishes Central Asia's importance for India. With India's partition, outreach to this region was hindered. Still, India enjoyed cordial relations with the region during Soviet times. With the collapse of the Soviet Union and the emergence of five independent republics- Kazakhstan, Kyrgyzstan, Tajikistan Turkmenistan and Uzbekistan; India's policy objectives were redefined.[2] Post-Independence, Central Asian countries sought viable partners in their economic and security areas. India's longstanding ties with the region provided an ideal opportunity for both sides to develop new and inventive ways to work together in the post-Soviet period.[3]

Of all the five Central Asia Republics (CARs), Tajikistan's is geo-strategically significant for India. Tajikistan shares a 1357 km long and porous border with Afghanistan; therefore, it has been prone to the regional security consequences arising from the Af-Pak region.[4] Considering the importance of the region, Indian Prime Minister Shri Atal Bihari Vajpayee visited Tajikistan in 2003. This visit was the first-ever visit by any Indian Prime Minister to Tajikistan. During this visit, the 'Extradition Treaty' and 'Agreement of Cooperation in the field of Terrorism' was signed.[5] This high-level visit was followed by President Smt. Pratibha Patil's visit to Dushanbe in 2009 and Vice President Shri Hamid Ansari in 2013.

Consistent bilateral high-level visits between the two countries have given impetus to bilateral cooperation. Tajik President Emomali Rahmon has visited India six times since 1995, and his recent state visit to India took place in December 2016.[6] Tajik President's visit to India in 2012 considered as a landmark in Indo-Tajik bilateral relations as both countries elevated their relationship to 'Strategic Partnership' to enhance cooperation on an extensive scale of areas including political, cultural, economy and trade, social welfare, defence, security, tourism and science and technology. During his official visit to the Central Asian region in July 2015, Prime Minister Modi visited Tajikistan and leaders of both countries discussed ways to accelerate cooperation in the field of defence, connectivity and combating terrorism.

In 2017, India's accession to the Shanghai Cooperation Organization (SCO) as a full member had substantiated the regularity in discussing issues of bilateral and multilateral importance. However, India's role in SCO is a matter of critical assessment about how India can make more use of this platform. For example, Indian businesses and industries need to be promoted at the SCO platform for greater cooperation with member countries. SCO can also be crucial for promoting India's cultural heritage (especially, Yoga) and educational potential.

India's concerns about the spread of Islamist extremism from the Af-Pak region has been an issue that brought India and Tajikistan closer since the mid-1990s. Moreover, US-led NATO forces withdrawal from Afghanistan in 2014 and afterwards led to uncertainty surrounding Afghanistan, which has further paved the way for collective security imperatives prioritizing India-Tajikistan ties. Pakistan's militants extended their support to the terrorist groups of Central Asia, such as the *Islamic Movement of Uzbekistan* (IMU) and *Hizb-ut-Tahrir* (HT). When the US launched its war on terror in Afghanistan in 2001, these militant groups fought alongside the Taliban. Having suffered heavy losses, they retreated to Pakistan's tribal areas and operated from there.[7]

This was considered a serious threat to Tajikistan's internal security. Moreover, the country's defence sector is still in an infantile stage, and the Russian Federation provides additional security to the Tajik-Afghan border. This is a common security challenge for New Delhi and Dushanbe, where they could act as a team on the counter-terrorism front, keeping aside geopolitical pressures and hesitations.

Political Relations

Diplomatic ties between India and Tajikistan were established in August 1992.[8] The convergence of economic, cultural, and security interests has enhanced cooperation in recent years. Consecutive visits from both sides accelerated the momentum of bilateral diplomatic and political relations. There are four key bilateral consultative mechanisms through which bilateral cooperation between Indian and Tajikistan is reviewed and discussed.

1. Foreign Office Consultations (fourth round of discussions were held on 19 December 2018, New Delhi),
2. Joint Working Group on Counter-terrorism (Third session held in June 2017, Dushanbe),

3. Joint Commission on Trade, Economic, Scientific and Technical Cooperation, (11th meeting was held on February 2020, New Delhi) and
4. Joint Working Group on Defence Cooperation (7th meeting was held on 26-27 July 2018, Dushanbe).
5. JWG on Peaceful Use of Space Technology for Development (the first meeting was held on 04 June 2019 through Direct Video Conferencing).

Speeding up of Trade and Economic Relations

Trade

India's total trade with Tajikistan is below the potential. Two-way trade between India and Tajikistan in 2020-21 was valued at a meagre 54.51 million USD which is 0.01 per cent of India's total trade for the same year. This consisted of India's exports to Tajikistan valued at 53.45 million USD and India's imports from Tajikistan worth 1.06 million USD. Indian exports mainly consist of pharmaceuticals, medical preparations, cane or beet sugar, tea, handicraft and machinery. Indian pharmaceutical products occupy approximately 25% of the Tajik market. Different types of ores, slag and ash, aluminium, organic chemicals, herbal oils, dried fruits and cotton are exported to India by Tajikistan.[9] India enjoys a trade surplus with Tajikistan however; export basket concerning Tajikistan needs to be expanded to enhance the bilateral economic cooperation.

India-Tajikistan Trade (in USD millions)

Year	2015-16	2016-17	2017-18	2018-19	2019-20	2020-21
Export	22.26	20.44	23.94	22.28	23.50	53.45
Import	9.98	21.82	50.29	4.24	0.29	1.06
Total Trade	32.24	42.26	74.24	26.52	23.80	54.51

Source: Dept of commerce, Government of India. https://tradestat.commerce.gov.in/eidb/iecnt.asp

To facilitate trade and investment with Dushanbe, Indian policymakers have fashioned an institutional framework. Intergovernmental Commissions (IGCs) for trade, economic, scientific, and technical cooperation were set up to explore the ways to expand trade and investments. Although these IGCs have been meeting regularly, the outcome has been minimal.[10] As proposed during the first India-Central Asia Dialogue, the 'India-Central Asia Business Council' was launched in February 2020 with the participation of apex commercial bodies of respective stakeholders, which can be seen as a stimulus to the economic engagement.[11]

Investments

To enhance Indian influence in Tajikistan, economic enterprising is a precondition. Tajikistan is interested in Indian investments in projects including energy, transportation, industry, agriculture, tourism, commerce and services, modern technology, and so forth. The country offers a lot of untapped investment potential. However, Indian business and commercial entities have been apprehensive about investing in the country due to the tough terrain. Tajikistan is rich in mineral resources. There is a huge opportunity for Indian investment in the mining sector of Tajikistan. Beijing has domination over this sector, but Chinese investment brings many challenges, from Chinese labour to debt trap and land grab. Tajikistan has been a victim of China's aggressiveness in the recent past when multiple Chinese websites circulated an article claiming the Pamir region to be part of China. India has goodwill within the Tajik population and leadership as well. Therefore, with concerted efforts and political will, New Delhi may win some of the mining projects in the country.

Some important Indian private investments/projects undertaken in Tajikistan include a 5-star hotel constructed by M/s CHL Limited, India, inaugurated by President Rahmon in September 2014. Under an Asian Development Bank (ADB) financed project, Indian company KEC/RPG, completed the construction of 116 km. long power transmission line from Sangtuda-1 Hydropower plant to Afghan border in October 2010. M/s Kalpataru, another Indian company, bagged a contract worth approximately USD 22 million to construct electric transmission lines under ADB financing. The project was finished in early 2017. The company won one more project worth around 70 million USD in 2017 under the CASA-1000 power transmission project.[12] Besides, other small private projects/companies/ clinics provide healthcare and other services in Tajikistan.[13]

Its vast energy resource potential will undoubtedly influence Tajikistan's economic growth. Tajikistan also hopes for expanding its collaboration in this area. The development of its hydroelectric potential, of which only 4 per cent is utilized, is a key goal of the Tajik Government. President Rahmon declared 2019 as the Year of Industrialization, creating opportunities for industrial firms to invest in Tajikistan. As an industrialized country, India can assist Tajikistan by sharing its knowledge and expertise in this area.[14]

India and Tajikistan share a rich cultural heritage; therefore, tourism development can complement the bilateral developmental partnership. India has a developed tourism sector so that it can contribute to the development of the tourism sector of Tajikistan. In the coming years, Tajikistan will also be able to use the credit line provided by India for the development of multiple sectors.

One critical factor contributing to limited Indian investment in Tajikistan and other Central Asian republics is a lack of adequate information. Many Indian and Central Asian businesspeople are unaware of the economic and commercial prospects present in the area. Trade events, fairs, and exhibits, for example, can provide a solid foundation for the growth of entrepreneurship between the two countries.

Connectivity

Another reason behind the negligible trade figures is the lack of direct access between both countries. The same scenario is visible in investments; India's business and investment projects in Tajikistan are a negligible two per cent. Until it fully connects with the region by railways, roads, or air corridors, economic cooperation will remain limited. India needs to shift the focus from an import oriented approach to establishing a manufacturing base in Central Asia. The Chabahar Port and the INSTC also remain crucial in this regard. Once fully operational, the Chabahar Port will enjoy an 8.5 million ton capacity.[15] To overcome the lack of connectivity and enhance trade between India and Tajikistan, Dushanbe fully supports the Chabahar Project, which provides adequate access to a seaport and makes it possible to enhance the economic and transit potential of Tajikistan.

The INSTC is a multi-modal transportation route linking the Indian Ocean and the Persian Gulf to the Caspian Sea via Iran, and onward to northern Europe via St. Petersburg in Russia. It will provide more direct access to Central Asia, Russia and Europe. At the same time, it will allow Iran and Azerbaijan to become regional transit hubs. The INSTC is to be 40 percent shorter and 30 percent cheaper than the traditional route taken through the Suez Canal.[16] It could help India, Iran, Central Asia and Russia to boost up their bilateral trade. There are at least three points (Sarakhs, Incheh-berun and Amirabad Port) on Iran's border with Central Asia which are connected to Bandar Abbas port by rail as well as road.[17] The existing infrastructure should be promoted by India, Iran and Central Asian republics for trade and business.[18]

Some new avenues to ensure connectivity between India and Central Asia need to be explored. The experience of the successful operationalization of the India-Afghanistan air corridor can be considered to further facilitate the extension of this corridor to Central Asia. India is engaged in promoting a dialogue on an air corridor between India and Central Asia. Both countries may together promote the connectivity initiatives for greater outreach and outcome. It will raise the confidence of the business communities in both countries to take up some fresh trade and investment initiatives.

Developmental Partnership and Capacity Building

As the geo-strategic importance of Tajikistan for India rose, India started to engage more deeply in building development partnerships with Tajikistan. Since 2006, Indian development assistance to Tajikistan amounted to INR 1.3 billion, given almost entirely as grants. Much of India's development assistance for Tajikistan has been directed towards developing power generation capacity and education. In addition to grants, India has also deepened its development partnership by disbursing Line of credit (LOCs) and budgetary loans.[19]

India extended its humanitarian assistance to Tajikistan during the Tajik Civil war by supplying food and related items.

In 2015 and 2017, India granted USD 100,000 to Tajikistan as humanitarian assistance for relief from natural disasters. In March 2018, India gifted ten ambulances to various regions of Tajikistan.[20] In October 2018, The President of India announced an allocation of USD 20 Million to Tajikistan to implement mutually identified and viable development projects.[21] Tajikistan is also one of the generously proportioned recipients of the ICCR (Indian Council of Cultural Relations) and ITEC (Indian Technical and Economic Cooperation) scholarship programmes outside the South Asian region.

Tajik applicants have received almost 1500 ITEC slots and 375 ICCR scholarships until now. For the financial year 2017-18, the Government of India provided sixty additional slots for customized training of Tajik experts in remote sensing.[22] The developmental partnership has added to the friendliness and mutual trust between the two countries. India needs to give more leverage to Tajikistan in terms of LOC and Grants especially for capacity building and infrastructure which has the potential to elevate the bilateral ties.

India-Tajikistan Relation: The Security Factor

Convergence of Interests in Countering Terrorism and Extremism

India and Tajikistan share similar concerns about extremism and terrorism, threatening these two secular and multi-ethnic states. Therefore, both trends and complexities in Afghanistan and Pakistan have security implications for both countries. If Afghanistan again falls to radical elements, Tajikistan would be the next target, and it will have spillover effects on other CARs. Likewise, radical activities in Afghanistan have also strategic implications for India. On the one hand, it would threaten Indian investments in Afghanistan and upsurge cross border terrorism in Jammu and Kashmir.[23]

The commonality of interests provides a greater opportunity to cooperate more closely in addressing the regional security issues. Pakistan's adamant position on sponsoring terrorism and providing safe havens to radical forces, re-emergence of Taliban in Afghanistan and withdrawal of US forces in 2014 and afterwards all are likely to have serious security implications for both countries. In this context, both countries underscored the need for enhanced cooperation to deal with these new security challenges in the region and ensured to work together towards combating terrorism and extremism through exchanging information, data and monitoring routes and finances of these radical forces.

India and Tajikistan have also emphasized on enhanced dialogue between their security agencies and regular meetings at the Foreign Ministers level to discuss the regional security issues. Moreover, coordinated efforts to work within the framework of the JWG on Combating International Terrorism and defence cooperation have also been significant development of their bilateral relations.[24]

Defence and Security

The scale of India's defence cooperation with Central Asian states has expanded to cover many areas ranging from military-to-military cooperation to the procurement of defence spares.[25] Defence cooperation between India and Tajikistan is considered one of the main pillars of their bilateral relations. India provides military training to many military officers and cadets from Tajikistan at its National Defence College and Indian Military Academy. India also set up India-Tajikistan Friendship Hospital near Qurganteppe, Tajikistan, where Indian doctors and medical staff provide medical care to the civil and arms forces patients. India also has extended material help and contribution to the military and security infrastructure of Tajikistan. India's cooperation with Tajikistan goes back to when both countries had extended support to Northern Alliance fighting against the Taliban in Afghanistan. In 2001, India had set up a small field hospital at Farkhor in Tajikistan, located near the Afghan border, ostensibly to treat the Northern Alliance fighters fighting against the Taliban.

Post-9/11, India made a bold strategic move to be militarily present in the region by undertaking renovation work of Ayni airbase in Tajikistan in 2002. This was a part of the bilateral initiative between India and Tajikistan, but India's first-ever initiative to take up a military project outside its territory could not materilaize due to geopolitical pressures on Tajikistan. The Ayni airbase was viewed as a substantial sign of India's determination to play a role in Central Asian security. It was also viewed as part of India's grand strategic thinking to be present at a vantage location to monitor conflict-torn Afghanistan and hostile activities by Pakistan vis-à-vis India, especially after the Kargil conflict.[26] Pakistan, an obvious protester to India's military endeavours in Central Asia was followed by both Russia and

China who also felt uncomfortable with New Delhi's desire to have a military base in Tajikistan. Consequently, Tajik Government on several occasions has ruled out of any possible Indian military deployment in its territory.[27] The refurbished Ayni airbase with 'state of the art navigational and defence technology' was formally opened in September 2010. Its runway was extended to approximately 3,200 meters with the intention that all types of aircraft can land there. [28]

External Factors

Strategically, the India-Central Asia relationship has been challenged by various powerful nations that seek to control the region. China and its belt and road initiative and Russia's attempts to retain influence in the region increase both risks and opportunities for India. Thus, India's attempts to rebuild its relationship with Central Asia are often viewed to counter China's presence in the region.[29] Moreover, as the competition between India and China intensifies, India also needs to push to gain the support of the Central Asian nations to attain a permanent seat in the United Nations Security Council (UNSC) and also a strategic position within the SCO. [30]

Central Asia is considered Russia's Sphere of Influence. Tajikistan is a member of Russia led Collective Security Treaty Organization (CSTO) and hosts more than 6,000 Russian troops deployed to the Russian Ground Forces' 201st military base in Tajikistan. Russia holds a strategic position in Dushanbe. However, ever-increasing Chinese penetration in the region will present an ultimate challenge to Russian interests. Moscow is India's trusted partner and all-weather allies; this could also help build a more constructive India-Russia partnership in Central Asia to balance Chinese influence.

The insecurities on the part of Islamabad are another concern affecting India's ties with Tajikistan. Pakistan has been extremely cautious of India's increasing influence in Central Asia and especially in Tajikistan. It has always been under this false impression that India's Central Asia policy aims to encircle Pakistan. Tajik President Emomali Rahmon paid a two-day visit to Pakistan on 2-3 June 2021, where he signed a defence agreement with Islamabad. According to this agreement, Pakistan would sell domestically manufactured arms to Dushanbe. Islamabad is trying to sell weapons to Tajikistan as part of its plan to expand its influence in Central Asia. It's venturing into selling arms in the Russian backyard may raise eyebrows in Moscow. Also, being a remittance dependent economy, Tajikistan lacks adequate funds; it will be interesting to see how Dushanbe pays for the arms purchase from Pakistan. Tajikistan-Pakistan defence deal should also be taken into reflection by policymakers in India.[31]

Conclusion

When one examines the diverse links that India and Tajikistan have cultivated over the year, one might certainly notice the mutual trust, respect, and confidence. However, by pursuing a more proactive Central Asia strategy, India may play a stronger role in Central Asia's economic and strategic domains. In recent years, there has been an upsurge in high-level contacts between the Indo-Tajik leadership. In 2017, India and Tajikistan celebrated the 25th anniversary of their diplomatic ties. The two countries' leaders also interact on different international platforms, such as the SCO, which provides them with additional opportunities to further their relationship.

India-Tajikistan relations have expanded cooperation in political, economic, cultural, military, and security areas. However, there is still a huge scope for increasing and diversifying their partnership through bilateral and multilateral mechanisms. The developments in Afghanistan following the failure of peace talks with the Taliban will have consequences for India and Tajikistan. As a result, both countries must work together with other Central Asian countries that share the same concerns to address the region's upcoming challenges.

India's engagement with Tajikistan is likely to enhance through several factors including, India's role in the development of Chabahar Port and INSTC, its membership of the SCO, and increased bilateral relations with each of the CARs. However, India has to develop a duel approach in dealing with the CARs; firstly, it has to look at the CARs as part of a consolidated geo-strategic space that is linked with other regions of Asia; secondly, India should independently deal with each of the CARs considering each republic's socio-political and economic peculiarities. This will lead to the success of Connect Central Asia policy in the true sense.

References

1 Chaturvedi H. (2017), India-Central Asian Links: Initial Probing in *Journal of Himalayan and Central Asian Studies*. Vol 21(4). Pp:3-18.

2 Joshi N. (2010). Introduction in Nirmala Joshi (ed) *Reconnecting India & Central Asia: Emerging Security & Economic Dimensions* (Central Asia Caucasus Institute: Johns Hopkins University, 2010), pp. 115-179.

3 Stobdan P. (2015). Central Asia: India's Northern Exposure', IDSA Monograph, No. 44. URl: https://idsa.in/system/files/monograph/monograph44.pdf.

4 Gupta PK (2021). Why are Central Asian countries wooing Pakistan? Article. Vivekananda International Foundation. July 15 2021. URl: https://www.vifindia.org/article/2021/july/15/why-are-central-asian-republics-wooing-pakistan

5 Joint Declaration on friendship and cooperation between the Republic of India and the Republic of Tajikistan, (2013 November 14).*Ministry of External Affairs Government of India.*URL: https://www.mea.gov.in/bilateral-documents.htm?dtl/7726/Joint_Declaration_on_friendship_and_cooperation_between_the_Republic_of_India_and_the_Republic_of_Tajikistan

6 Tajik President Emomali Rahmon to visit India (2016 December 8). *The Business Standard.* URL: https://www.business-standard.com/article/news-ians/tajik-president-emomali-rahmon-to-visit-india-116120801270_1.html

7 Witter D. (2011). Uzbek militancy in Pakistan's tribal region. Backgrounder. Institute for the study of war. URL: http://www.understandingwar.org/sites/default/files/BackgrounderIMU_28Jan.pdf

8 Bakshi J. (2013). India and Tajikistan: Common Concerns and Shared Interests in Evolving Regional Geopolitics in *Geopolitical Dynamics in India-Tajikistan Relations*, (Eds.), Jyotsna Bakhshi, Pentagon Press.

9 'India – Central Asia Trade: Roots of Strong Economic Relationship', Research Bureau PHD Chamber of Commerce and Industry, August 2017. https://www.phdcci.in/wp-content/uploads/2018/12/India_Central-Asia-Trade_Roots-of-Strong-Economic-Relationship-August-2017.pdf.

10 Pradhan R. (2015). 'India's Soft Power in Central Asia: Why it Must Act on the Look North Policy', Mainstream, Vol. 3 (29), July 11, 2015. http://www.mainstreamweekly.net/article5792.html.

11 Gupta PK (2020). 'India-Central Asia Business Council: Reinvigorating India-Central Asia Economic Engagement' VIF Commentary, February 10, 2020. https://www.vifindia.org/2020/february/10/india-central-asia-business-council

12 Central Asia-South Asia (CASA-1000) Electricity Transmission Project. NS Enrgy. https://www.nsenergybusiness.com/projects/casa-1000-electricity-transmission/

13 'Bilateral Relations and Visits' (2020), Embassy of India, Dushanbe, Tajikistan URL: http://www.eoidushanbe.gov.in/page/bilateral-relations-and-visits/

14 Jaishankar says huge potential for further strengthening Indo-Tajik economic cooperation (2021 March 31). *DT Next.* URL: https://www.dtnext.in/News/TopNews/2021/03/31164849/1284324/Jaishankar-says-huge-potential-for-further-strengthening-.vpf

15 Iran inaugurates extension to strategic Chabahar Port; new piers to triple its capacity (2017 December 3). *Firstpost.* URL: https://www.firstpost.com/world/iran-inaugurates-extension-to-strategic-chabahar-port-new-piers-to-tri-

ple-its-capacity-4239883.html

16 Gupta PK (2020), Summary of Discussions, VIF Roundtable on India-Central Asia Relations, URL: https://www.vifindia.org/sites/default/files/VIF-Roundtable-on-India-Central-Asia-Relations.pdf

17 Ibid.

18 Ibid.

19 Mullen R. and Prasad. (2014). India-Tajikistan brief, Centre for Policy Research. http://cprindia.org/sites/default/files/policy-briefs/India-Tajikistan%20Brief%20Final.pdf

20 'Bilateral Relations and Visits' (2020), Embassy of India, Dushanbe, Tajikistan URL: http://www.eoidushanbe.gov.in/page/bilateral-relations-and-visits/

21 MEA, Joint statement after the Indian President visit to Tajikistan in October 2018, URL:

https://www.mea.gov.in/bilateraldocuments.htm?dtl/30482/IndiaTajikistan_Joint_Statement_during_State_Visit_of_President_to_Tajikistan_79_October_2018

22 'Bilateral Relations and Visits' (2020), Embassy of India, Dushanbe, Tajikistan URL: http://www.eoidushanbe.gov.in/page/bilateral-relations-and-visits/

23 Sharma R. (2014). A Perspective on India-Tajikistan Strategic Partnership, United Service institute of India. URL: http://usiofindia.org/Article/Print/?pub=Journal&pubno=598&ano=2756

24 Roy M S (2012), India and Tajikistan: Building a long-term Strategic Partnership. IDSA Comments. https://idsa.in/idsacomments/IndiaandTajikistan-BuildingalongtermStrategicPartnership_MeenaSRoy_180912

25 Ibid.

26 Stobdan P. (2020). India and Central Asia: The Strategic Dimension', IDSA Monograph. KW Publishers New Delhi.

27 Putz C. (2015). Will There Be an Indian Air Base in Tajikistan?. The Diplomat. 15 July 2015. URL: https://thediplomat.com/2015/07/will-there-be-an-indian-air-base-in-tajikistan/

28 Tajikistan- Air force. Global Security. URL: https://www.globalsecurity.org/military/world/centralasia/tajik-airforce.htm

29 Jiang, Y. (2020). Russia's Strategy in Central Asia: Inviting India to Balance China, The Diplomat, January 23, 2020. URL: https://thediplomat.com/2020/01/russias-strategy-in-central-asia-inviting-india-to-balance-china/

30 Ibid.

31 Gupta PK (2021). Why are Central Asian countries wooing Pakistan? Article. Vivekananda International Foundation. July 15 2021. URl: https://www.vifindia.org/article/2021/july/15/why-are-central-asian-republics-wooing-pakistan

7. A Fiddle, A Horse and A Bodhi Tree Sapling: The Role of Soft Power Diplomacy in Indo Mongolian Relations

Anagha Babu[1]

Abstract

The soft power diplomacy of India and its potential are fertile grounds for research and deliberations. Indian soft power has been of enormous advantage for its foreign policy. The prospect of India becoming a world power today is considered a possibility due to its vast and varied soft power elements and the Indian efforts to shed off the Third World tag. Though criticised at times for its social inequalities and poverty, India has successfully portrayed itself as a nation of rich culture, history, heritage and unique philosophy. Though blessed with necessary and essential tools to become the pioneer in the soft power arena, India yet has not fully explored its potential. This paper examines the role of India's soft power in Indo-Mongolian relations. This paper is divided into four sections. Section one deals with the sources of India's soft power in general. Section two examines the role of soft power in bilateral relations between India and Mongolia. The third and fourth sections looks into the conclusion and policy recommendations in the discussed arena and suggestions for improving Indian soft power diplomacy.

Keywords: Mongolia, India, Culture, Buddhism, Soft Power, Diplomacy, Foreign Policy

Introduction

Joseph Nye, the Harvard professor who proposed and propagated the concept in the1980s defined soft power as 'the ability to attract people to our side without

1 Anagha Babu is an Assistant Professor at Kumaraguru College of Liberal Arts and Science, Coimbatore, India.

coercion' (Nye, 2004). Since then, the concept has caught on and much scholarly work has been done on it. If certain historical texts are to be believed Genghis Khan had dropped his aspirations for expansion into India following warnings of the scorching Indian summers. This Mongol dream was realized in the 14th century through Ghengis's son in law Timur's descendant Babur who had laid the foundations of the Mughal empire (Dasgupta, 2019).

The Buddhist tendencies in Mongolia paved way to then renewed Indian interests in the region and over the years this has reinforced the Indo-Mangolian ties apart from the historical, economic, infrastructural, educational and cultural endeavours in bilateral ties in the more than 8000 years old Indo Mangolian relationship.

Many describe the Indo Mongolian ties to be more than 10000 years old and for them, 'Indians from the Kangra kingdom in the Himalayan foothills migrated to the present territory of Mongolia' (Nyamdavaa, 2015). The mission was led by Mangaldev, the prince of the kinngdom. Their descendants are believed to have returned to India after 2000 years. Their hereditary leader is the head of the Katoch[2] dynasty, the descendants at present in Himachal Pradesh and Rajasthan. Former Prime Minister of Mongolia, Anandyn Amar in his book *Short History of Mongolia* showed references and stated that the 'Mongolian forefathers came from south of the Himalayas' (Nyamdavaa, 2015). Many words in the South Indian Dravidian languages have resemblances with the words and their edifice in Mongolian language. *Alikali* is an extraordinary manual of Sanskrit with Tibetan and Mongolian translations, which has served as a textbook in Mongolian monasteries for centuries' (Nyamdavaa, 2015). For India and its neighbourhood, the first investigative assessment to evaluate Indian cultural, historical and literary links vis a vis Mongolia was initiated under the tutelage of Professor Raghu Vira and with the assistance of Mongolian language expert M Dugersuren. This association had set a strong base for the diplomatic ties between the states. Soft power diplomacy in Indo Mangolian associations was evident much before the diplomats and embassies were instituted.

Indian Soft Power

Indian soft power is now finding larger application in public diplomacy. Elements of India's art and cultural heritage and architecture involving aspects of films, dance, music, painting, philosophy, yoga, mysticism, traditional knowledge and literature have brought India closer to many world nations. Yoga has now become a way of life. In almost all the nations, the International day of Yoga, June 21st is witnessed not only as the means for physical well-being, but also as a celebration of the

2 A Rajput dynasty in India

Indian art and culture. Indian political values and social concepts which promote equality, fraternity, social inclusion, and democratic values tend to boost the image of India abroad. India's foreign policy that respects and promotes international co-operation and acknowledges the role of international organization in achieving the same and ensuring international peace has given it the image of a leader in the age of democracy. Even though it was an underprivileged country, India became the leader of the third world and of the Non-Aligned Movement during the Cold War mostly due to its soft power. The legacy of not entering in wars and violence and being a non-aggressive nation, made India a friend of many. The neighbours in the region were once part of India, while the extended neighbourhood, especially in South East India and Central Asia, were influenced by the Indian culture, history and heritage which got transported to the region through trade and political conquests. The similarity of cuisines of Central Asia and India is a demonstration of the same (Khanna, 2014). A major export item along the classical Indian Ocean trade routes was religious thought and philosophy, especially the ideas of Buddhism, Hinduism and Jainism spread through the merchants and trade relations rather than missionaries and wars alone. These political, cultural, and economic advents turned to be effective in building relations with the immediate and extended neighbourhood in the region.

The most important and effective instrument for soft power is the Indian diaspora. The respect and command it enjoys in the resident countries can help the Indian government in the execution of policies. Canada, USA, Britain, and Ireland are a few of the nations where individuals of Indian origin playing influential and crucial roles in administration and governance. What makes the Indian diaspora unique and desirable is the skill and education that proves beneficial to the host country. Globalisation and the advancement of science and technology have further made the Indian diaspora appreciated by the international community.

The change in the economic aspirations and attitudes of India since 1991 has influenced the global acceptance of India as a partner in economic integration and development. The International Monetary Fund says India is on the road to become one of the top five economies in the world by 2030 (India's Strong Economy Continues to Lead Global Growth, 2018). Indian innovations, technology and scientific accomplishments have surprised the world. India's technological advancement— especially in the area of space and nuclear energy has been a shock for many and surprise for a few nations. 'It is emerging as the fifth or sixth of the leading space powers in the fifth or sixth of the leading space powers in the world' (Nayar & Paul, 2013, p. 134). The success of the Mars Orbiter Mission (MOM) and Chandrayan has further ratified the Indian advancement in the field of astronomy. Dinshaw Mistry attributes the Indian rise in space science as one of toil, research and constructive criticism and believes 'only Israel and Brazil are likely to follow

India's evolutionary route to advanced satellite-launch capability' (Mistry, 1998, p. 156). The Indian Technical and Economic Cooperation (ITEC) programme initiated by the Ministry of External Affairs in 1964, should be seen as an Indian attempt to harness power by aiming at economic growth of the South Asian region and beyond through mutual cooperation and trade (Chandavarkar, 1972). Though initially the programme was focussing on South Asian and Central Asian nations, the extended purview has now brought African and East European nations too under the programme which points at economic power used to establish relations and cooperation; a clear example of economic activities being transformed as agents of soft power.

With regard to Mongolia and Indian soft power, the trump card is Buddhism and faith diplomacy that is aligned with it. The faith diplomacy was effectively used while the bodhi tree sapling reached *Ulaanbaatar* and when Indian Prime Minister visited the *Gandan* and other Buddhist monasteries. The Mongolians reciprocated with introducing Narendra Modi to *morin khuur*[3] and the gifting the Mongolian horse *Kanthaka*[4]. India tried to recuperate the cultural and historical relations by also presenting the *Jamiat Tawarikh*[5]. The participation of Narendra Modi in the Naadam[6] festival and the dressing in the traditional Mongolian attire deel has shown the importance of including cultural diplomacy and soft power tools while engaging with foreign states. The Mongolian and foreign media encouraged these activities and images were widely shared from the official handles of Indian PM, the Indian ministers and Mongolian leaders. The present is easy because of the past. The next section points to the Indian soft power diplomacy in Mongolia from the earlier times.

Indo Mongolian Relations

India is an example of a civilization having strong 'Hindu-Buddhist foundations,

3 A traditional Mongolian two-stringed fiddle which is adorned with a carved horse head (In Mongolia, Modi tries his hand on the morin khuur, 2015)

4 This was the name of the horse of Prince Siddhartha (pre monastic name of Lord Buddha)

5 This is a work of literature and history, produced in the Mongol Ilkhanate (Southern west empire in Mongolia). It was authored by Rashid-al-Din Hamadani at the start of the 14th century. The breadth of coverage of the work has caused it to be called "the first world history". Mongolia had lost this resource narrating its past during the Communist regime. Professor Raghu Vira helped in attaining its copy and thus aided in the preservation of a rare piece of history. There are references to India also in the text.

6 The traditional festival of Mongolia with a focus on three traditional games in the region — archery, horse racing and wrestling. It is also referred to as the called the world's second-oldest Olympics.

centuries of Islamic influence, and integration with Western institutions and ideas', thus equipping India with cultural elements to 'deal with the diverse, globalized and complex realities of the twenty-first century' (Thussu, 2019).

12th century saw the influence of Indian political system in Mongolia as during this period the Mongol rulers preferred to be greeted as *Chakravartin*[7] *Khan*. There is a Sanskrit influence witnessed in many Mongol names even today. Though Buddhism reached Mongolia through Tibet, the Indian associations with Buddhism have been effective tools in establishing soft power diplomacy between India and Mongolia. The Mongol Buddhists heading to Nalanda[8] for lessons and honouring India as the land of Buddha was an impetus for opening the doors of public diplomacy in Mongolia. 'The incarnate of the last Mongol theocratic ruler Khalka Jebdtsundamba[9]' whose identity was kept a secret by even Dalai Lama, had lived in India working even in radio stations until he died in 2012 (Stobdan, 2015).

India struggled for Mongolia's UN membership and independence in 1961. Krishna Menon, who was the then Indian ambassador to the United Nations said, "Mongolia was founded not today, but existed as an independent state over many centuries" (Wangchuk, 2018). India had engaged in diplomatic endeavours with Mongolia since 1955. Reciprocating the Indian values of friendship and relations, Mongolia along with Bhutan began the UN resolution for the cause of Bangladesh's independence. The actions by India and Mongolia were detrimental to the interests of China and Pakistan respectively.

'The Mongolian equivalent of the 'colour revolution' was inspired by Indian wisdom; people then chose the Buddhist path for transforming Asia's first Communist state into a democratic society' (Stobdan, 2015). This led to initiation of new diplomatic strategies by India to engage with Mongolia. Kushak Bakula Rinpoche of Ladakh served as India's envoy to Mongolia for a decade from 1990, and was engrossed in convalescing Buddhism for Mongolia that was coming out of the communist regime. Mongolia considers Buddhism as 'the link between its past and present and exists as an upholder of the Mongolian way of life' (Dasgupta, 2019). The best illustration for this is the relevance of Genghis Khan as a figure of Mahayana Buddhism in Mongolia. They see him as the reincarnation of the *Bodhisattva Vajrapani*[10]. Genghis Khan who similar to the fellow herders in the

---

7 A term in Sanskrit/ Hindi/ Dravidian languages meaning Emperor in English

8 A historic university at Bihar built during the Gupta period that had housed Buddhist scholars from abroad and parts of India alike, destroyed by Khilji dynasty and now revived and functioning at Rajgir. To know more about the history of the institution refer https://nalandauniv.edu.in/about-nalanda/history-and-revival/

9 Is the salutation for the theocratic leader of Mongolia; similar to Dalai Lama of Tibet. He is the third highest Lama in Tibetan Buddhism.

10 Buddhist saviour from the seventh century or soon after. Vajrapani, the "holder of

region, worshipped natural elements especially the blue sky and Mount Burkhan Khaldun[11](Religious and cultural parallels can be drawn in India during early Vedic era and Indus valley civilsation). This is an example that attempts to connect to the pre–Buddhist Mongolian culture. This has been effective for Indian soft power. The elephant-headed Ganesh, Saraswati and Yama represented by two walking skeletons were some of the references from this era (having paralells with Indian culture) that have been revived due to this. The pet eagle of Genghis Khan was named *Garid*[12]. The prehistoric cultural ties have been thus revived.

Indian literature is highly appreciated in Mongolia. Kalidasa's *Meghdoota Astangahridaya Samhita* of Vagbhata is translated in Mongolian and they follow it (Chandra, 2016). Texts like *Panchtantra*[13], *Ramayana*[14], *Shakuntala*[15], *Ritu Samhara*[16], *Kamasutra*[17], *Godaan*[18], *Gaban*[19] , important Indian Buddhist scriptures and even *Kati Patang*[20] and have been published in Mongolian language. Amitabh Bachchan is loved dearly in the land of Genghis Khan. Bollywood had a strong fan base in Mongolia, though the young generation now prefers Hollywood movies dubbed in Russian to the Hindi movies poorly dubbed in Russian. Indian movies and shows dubbed in Mongolian are appreciated as Russian as a language is losing its prominence in Mongolia. Mahabharata, being broadcast on Ulaanbaat TV dubbed in Mongolian has decent viewership (Report, 2013). The Changezi Chicken[21], named after the celebrated father figure of Mongolia is very popular in India especially in Uttar Pradesh and Delhi (Daniyal, 2015). This was found fascinating by the Mongolian President Khaltmaagiin Battulga when he

---

a thunderbolt" (vajra), shares his origins with the Vedic deity Indra, God of storms (MET, n.d.).

11 The mountain in Northern Mongolia and its locality is believed to be the birthplace of Genghis Khan as well as his tomb.

12 A reference could be made to the mystical bird 'Garud' in ancient Indian scriptures. Garid is also the rank given in ancient Mongolian wrestling.

13 The Panchatantra is an ancient Indian collection of interrelated animal fables in Sanskrit verse and prose, arranged within a frame story, written by Vishnu Sharma between 1200 – 300 CE (Tale, n.d.).

14 Ancient Indian epic written by Valmiki describing the life Lord Ram.

15 A character from Indian epic Mahabharata on whom Kalidasa based his work Abhijnanashakuntalam

16 The work of Kalidasa mentioning seasons

17 The Kama Sutra is an ancient Indian Sanskrit text authored by Vatsyayana dealing with sexuality, eroticism and emotional fulfilment in sex life.

18 A famous Hindi novel authored by Munshi Premchand

19 A major Hindi novel by Munshi Premchand

20 A Hindi novel by Gulshan Nanda. A Bollywood movie is also present with the same title.

21 A dish having roasted chicken in a tomato gravy

visited India in 2019. He came with a 'high-level delegation comprising of senior officials and businessmen with a rich itinerary and interactions' who partook in the India –Mongolia Business Forum (Trigunayat, 2019). Along with investments and business opportunities 'Mongolia also hopes to be a hub for some Indian companies and would like to benefit from rural communication technologies to connect its sparsely located population' (Trigunayat, 2019). Mongolia wants to explore its solar power potential and as India has emerged a major player and leader of the International Solar Alliance[22], assistance is expected in this arena too.

There are evidences of shared heritage between India and Mongolia. A coin excavated from Mathura belonging to the second century BCE has an inscription of the Mongolian word *Khagan* meaning emperor. The well-known linguist and cultural studies scholar Prof Raghu Vira along with Mongolian professor Rinchin, tried to revive Mongolian literature, culture and the Indo-Mongol historical and cultural ties. As a result the International Congress of Mongolistics (Mongolian Studies) was held in 1959 in Mongolia. In 1956, when Mongolians celebrated Buddha Jayanti in India, they returned to Mongolia with the water from Ganges, thus commemorating the 17th century Buddhist teachers who reached Mongolia not only with water from Ganga (which was later added to Lake Baikhal), but also tales of Lord Krishna, King Bhoja and Vikram-Betaal.

The India-Mongolian Agreement on Cultural Cooperation signed in 1961 also put forward a Cultural Exchange Programme (CEP) between the two countries. Indo Mongolian relations have witnessed a surge since 1973, 'when it signed an eight-point joint declaration, which became the basis for cooperation between the two countries' (Ananth, 2015). The Treaty of Friendly Relations and Cooperation signed in 1994 on the backdrop of Mongolian president Ochirbat's visit, further strengthened this new found thrust in the bilateral ties of these states strengthened further by joint declarations in 2001, 2004 and 2009. In June 2019 at the Asian Buddhist Conference on Peace (ABCP), a Laddakh Mask Dance troupe performed. 'There are regular exchanges of cultural troupes and performances of Indian performing groups that are well appreciated in Mongolia' (Report, 2021). 'The CEP was renewed in 2003, 2005, 2009 and 2015 and most recently in September 2019 during the visit of Mongolian President until 2022' (Report, 2021). Since 2000 an Indian dance competition titled '*Melody of Ganga*' for Mongolian school children is being organized by Indian Cultural Centre and the Indian embassy at Mongolia. The event was not conducted in 2020 owing to Covid -19.

---

22 It was conceived as a coalition of solar-resource-rich countries (which lie either completely or partly between the Tropic of Cancer and the Tropic of Capricorn) to address their special energy needs in 2015 with headquarters in Gurugram, India (ISA, n.d.).

The government of India deserves special appreciation for curating the cultural ties in Indo Mongolian ties. The act of conferring an honorary doctorate on former Mongolian Prime Minister Nambariin Enkhbayar in 2004 'for his role in promoting democracy and Buddhism' is just one among examples of the same (Stobdan, 2015). Through such strategic moves India opened its avenues for engagements in Northeast Asia. The first Mongolian Buddhist Monastery saw its foundation being laid in Bodh Gaya during the regime of Atal Bihari Vajpayee. This is sustained in the engagements of Modi government.

Hindu Kush Himalayan region is often referred to as the third pole, — the first and second being north and south poles, — as it is the world's largest storehouse of snow and ice after the polar region. The World Meteorological Organisation has indicated its faith in the Indian cause of climate protection when it has requested for Indian action in the region, sharing the supervisory role with Pakistan and China (Koshy, 2019)

Narendra Modi in his 2015 visit to Mongolia signed the declaration of 'Strategic Partnership', ratified a 22-point Joint Statement, announced USD 1 Billion Line of Credit for Infrastructure advancement in Mongolia (building of 1st Oil Refinery) and inked 13 agreements[23] in diverse fields. The Memorandums of Understanding signed in 2019 between India and Mongolia in the fields of 'cooperation and usage of outer space for civilian purposes' and disaster management further validate that the bilateral ties are to be further pursued (Express, 2019). India has initiated a pitch for enhanced economic cooperation with Mongolia, aiming to stymie the Chinese interests and influence in the region developed primarily due to the economic assistance from China. The Indian Prime Minister by addressing the Mongolian Parliament (in 2015) on a Sunday became the only foreign dignitary to address the State Great Khural[24] on a holiday. Mongolia had supported India's proposal to Yoga's inscription into the list of UNESCO's Intangible Cultural Heritage while India reciprocated by voting for the 'Mongolian Traditional Custom to Worship Mountain and Ovoo[25]' to be included in the list of Intangible Cultural Heritage.

23 Agreement on Transfer of Sentenced Prisoners, Revised Air Services Agreement, Agreement on Cooperation in the field of Animal Health and Dairy, MOU on establishment of a Joint India-Mongolia Friendship School, MOU on cooperation in the area of Traditional Systems of Medicine, Cultural Exchange Program for 2015-18, MOU on Cooperation in the field of Border Patrolling & Surveillance, MOU on cooperation between National Security Councils, and MOU on gifting a Bhabatron-II Cancer Therapy Machine (implemented) to the National Cancer Centre in Ulaanbaatar (Report, Brief on India-Mongolia Bilateral Relations, 2020).

24 The Mongolian Parliament

25 There are ten mountains recognised by the Mongolian government for worship as a part of commemorating the ancient 'Mongolian culture and tradition of protecting, loving and worshipping the mother-nature' and to live in high awareness of essential

Indian Prime Minister Modi on the day of Buddha Purnima stated "without Buddha, the 21st century would not be the Asian Century" thus again invoking the traits of faith diplomacy (Soni, 2016).

Polo in its latest form could trace its origin back to India, to be precise, modern day Manipur. The British discovered the princes of Manipur playing a game similar to hockey on horsebacks and were entranced by it. This led to the setting up of first polo club in the world, the Silchar Kangjei Club in Assam. This had taken Polo further to its present popularity, now widely played and recognised across more than 70 countries. The polo matches between women players of India and countries like US, Australia and Kenya were conducted in 2018 under the supervision of Indian Polo Association and Huntre! Equine[26] (Bahl, 2019). Mongolia with his vast steppes and love for horses has the perfect setting for Polo. Genghis Khan had stimulated his cavalry to engage in the sport, a prototype of Polo, which later dwindled in popularity. Since the past decade attempts by the Mongolian Polo Club and Genghis Khan Polo Club has promoted polo among Mongolian youth. Competitions at international level in Polo were conducted by these clubs in Mongolia. India and Huntre!Equine can align with Mongolia to revamp Polo and thus start new trajectories in sports diplomacy.

Jawaharlal Nehru and now Narendra Modi have proudly reinforced and accredited the 'cultural ownership of the shared Indo- Mongolian heritage' (Stobdan, 2015). Narendra Modi's visit to Ulaanbaatar to celebrate the diamond jubilee of Indo-Mongolian ties and 25 years of Mongolian democracy in 2015 is yet another effective step in endorsing the Indian soft power diplomacy in the region. The 'Nomadic Elephant[27]' and the expected increase in uranium imports are outcomes of the soft power endeavours to an extent.

The aim of the Nomadic Elephant exercise, for the Indian Army 'is to boost inter-operability between the two armies and strengthen cooperation in the areas of counter insurgency and counter terrorism'; which is in prospective of keeping Chinese interventions along Mongolian borders at bay (Parameswaran, 2016).

Indian Council for Cultural Relations is providing scholarships for Mongolian students to study in Indian universities and thereby encouraging opportunities for cultural exchange. This is an effective step towards creating a conducive public opinion for India among Mongolians and generating future Mongolian leaders with

---

bonds between the nature and human being'. (Studio.M, 2016)

26 Huntre! Equine is an organisation that has aimed towards finding close links between sports and culture and encouraging policy framers for using the same as tools for constructive diplomatic endeavours (Huntre! Equine, n.d.)

27 The Military exercise between India and Mongolia focussing on countering terrorism

Indian alignment and interests. ICCR has also donated 14 sets of *Kanjurs*[28] *(Urga & Narthang)* to the Mongolian government. All the 108 volumes of the Mongolian Kanjur are expected to be similarly completed and published by 2022. Apart from these '21 volumes of Indian classic literature have been translated into Mongolian language by Dr. Gendendarm and were published with financial assistance from ICCR' (Report, 2020). In 2019 Dr Shirendev, a Mongolian Indologist 'translated 8 volumes of 'Dhammpada" from Pali into Mongolian language'. (Report, 2020). Every year four students are selected from the students studying Hindi at the classes conducted by the Indian mission at Mongolia to study Hindi at Kendriya Hindi Sansthan, Agra on scholarship

The establishment of Rajiv Gandhi College for Production and Art (Turbat, 2020)and the Atal Bihari Vajpayee Centre of Excellence (ABVCE) in Information and Communication Technology (ICT) initiated in Mongolia named after former Indian prime Ministers, aiming at skill enhancement and training in various fields is an illustration of science diplomacy; an effective variant of Indian soft power diplomacy.

Modi has become the political leader second to Barack Obama with highest followers in social media, especially Twitter; providing the Indian government enhanced reach to an enormous global audience, as per the June 2021 survey of the leaders with most number of followers in Twitter (Boyd, 2021). The appearance of Indian diplomats and politicians in twitter and social media platforms is an added catalyst to twitter diplomacy. While meeting the Mongolian President Battulga on background of the Shanghai Cooperation Organisation[29] in 2019 and after few months during the 5th Far Eastern Economic Forum [30]in Vladivostok, the friendship and personal quotients were again strengthened. The friendships

28 It is the most important religious text in Mongolia. It is held in high esteem by the Mongolian Buddhists and they worship the Kanjur at temples. It is kept almost in every monastery in Mongolia. The.Mongolian Kanjur translated from Tibetan to the Classical Mongolian is a source of Mongolian culture too. During the communist rule, all these were destroyed by Soviet Union and it was Professor Raghu Vira who had obtained a microfilm copy of the rare Kanjur manuscripts in 1956-58, and brought them to India. This is now being translated, printed and given to Mongolia (Culture, 2020)

29 The Shanghai Cooperation Organisation (SCO) is a permanent intergovernmental international organisation focussing on the economic development Asian nations especially Central Asian countries and its neighbours which was formed in 2001 and has headquarters at Beijing, China (SCO, n.d.).

30 The Eastern Economic Forum was established by decree of the President of the Russian Federation Vladimir Putin in 2015 to support the economic development of Russia's Far East and to expand international cooperation in the Asia-Pacific region (EEC, n.d.).

of national leaders would reflect in the bilateral ties too. PM Modi took to twitter and posted "Engaging with a cherished spiritual friend and developmental partner. Held talks with Mr Khaltmaagiin Battulga, the President of Mongolia. We reviewed the full range of bilateral ties and deliberated on ways to enhance cooperation for the mutual benefit of our people" (PMO, @narendramodi, 2019). In his 2015 visit to Mongolia during the Naadam festival, the cultural symbols of both Mongolia and India were very evident in his tweets. Dressed in the traditional Mongolian attire — 'deel' and posing with a Mongolian horse, he tweeted "With Kanthaka, a gift from Mongolia" (PMO, 2015). "Steppes pe charcha! PM and PM Saikhanbileg deep in conversation during the Mini-Naadam Festival" is how described the photo of the Mongolian Prime Minister Chimed Saikhanbileg and Indian Prime Minister in the backdrop of Mongolian mountains in traditional Mongolian deel was described by Arindam Bagchi (MEA Spokesperson) through the twitter handle @MEAIndia. The photos of the visit to the vital Buddhist monasteries in Mongolia, presenting the Bodh Gaya tree sapling and the copy of *Jamiat Tawarikh* apart from the selfies with Mongolian President Tsakhiagiin Elbegdorj were franticly shared across social media from the official @narendramodi twitter handle. All the above mentioned tweets and social media presence have received encouraging responses from majority of the citizens of Mongolia, other Central Asian countries and India. The Indo Mongolian relations has received a constructive impetus under twitter diplomacy, selfie diplomacy and hug diplomacy— all novel variants of soft power.

Conclusion and Way Forward

'With a double-digit growth, Mongolia today is one of the fastest growing economies in the world' (Soni, 2016). The recently received pseudonym *Minegolia* owing to the sudden boom in the mining sector - especially in uranium, gold, coal and copper, Mongolia is listed among the top ten countries with respect to its natural resources. Indian engagements with Mongolia should be conceived and designed keeping these in mind. India could start by deliberately concentrating on aiding Mongolia in its 'broad-based inclusive growth, which demands sustainable and effective management of the vast natural resources' which is already practiced by Indo Mongolian policy makers (Soni, 2016). For Mongolia India is not only one of the most trusted partners but also a 'spiritual neighbour'. The faith diplomacy and cultural diplomacy are the best forms of soft power variants that should be sharpened while India engages with Mongolia.

It is evident that the Indian interests and aspirations are encouraged by Mongolia. India can be a probable successful market for 'Mongolia's evolved cashmere knitwear industry, and they can benefit from India's information technology services and scholarships to students (Dasgupta, 2019). It is crucial that the 'soft power linkages between the two civilizations must proceed autonomously' encouraging the foreign policy to concentrate on a 'civilizational dimension' (Dasgupta, 2019)

Indian and Mongolian scholars must be encouraged to absorb in research focussing on the legends, traditions and archives recording the bilateral ties of the countries and the acquired knowledge should be taught in colleges and universities (Nyamdavaa, 2015). "India for world Buddhism" is a successful approach for diplomatic and cultural outreach pursuits. It is apparent that the 'current economic, political and people-to-people relations between Mongolia and India are based on old links' has established a compact ground for the future of Indo Mangolian relations. This could be better incorporated if the Indian and Mongolian younger generations are introduced to the cultural, historical and literacy associations between the two countries. An Asian cultural forum or centre could be set up 'based on similar cultures, traditions and ways of thinking shared across the continent' (Nyamdavaa, 2015).

Mongolia is an emerging power with strategic relevance in the region. There are many reasons facilitating this finding. Mongolia is a 'good neighbour' as it does not indulge in territorial or border disputes, and has amiable relations with the immediate and extended neighbourhood including with the two Koreas. The Mongolian proverb 'a duck is calm when the sea is calm' guides the Mongolian policies and hence Mongolia believes that its interests are 'best served when the environment is predictable and stable' (Enkhsaikhan, 2014). This is what prompts Mongolia to initiate deliberations and discussion forums among the countries in the region. To display that 'small states can be active players and can make a significant contribution to strengthening regional peace and security', Mongolia is adamant to uphold its nuclear weapon free status (Enkhsaikhan, 2014). Mongolia is striding towards being a strong soft power and India should leave no stones unturned in being a partner in the process.

Mongolia is India's most accessible and robust pivot to the Eurasian affairs. The 'third neighbour policy[31]' of Mongolia has been fruitful for Indian interests in Central Asia. Though acknowledged that the Chinese speedy expeditions have public incompatibilities in Mongolia giving rise to strong anti-Chinese feelings in the state especially over 'China's major resource development projects, extraction of minerals like coal and copper in Tavan Tolgoi and Oyu Tolgoi in Gobi deserts', yet the Mongolian government is convinced of the economic and infrastructural

31 In 1990 the then US secretary of state James Baker in his speech to the Great Khural, used the term "third neighbour doctrine", which initially applied to the United States and the West at large, reflecting to the idea of engaging with countries out of the immediate neighbourhood. Mongolia has used this doctrine as a base for its increased associations with India, Germany, Australia and Japan in the past decade apart from the US.

developments that China provides as there is no possible replacement for the same (Stobdan, 2015). India should focus on the initiations started earlier in 2006 between Indian Border Security Force (BSF) and the Mongol General Authority of Border Protection (GABP) with added attention and emphasis on buttressing the Mongolian capabilities to check its Chinese borders. The situation is aptly explained in the following lines

> The Mongols may not like the Chinese, but in reality they cannot live without the Chinese. And while the Mongols love Indians, they can live without India. That is why Modi should just work on strengthening Indian influence in Mongolia because that is something the Chinese cannot buy through their money.
>
> –In Modi's Mongolia Pivot, a Test of Indian Soft Power (Stobdan, 2015)

Recommendations for Augmenting Indian Soft Power in General

The productive economic standards and 'a youthful demography' along with the democratic practices and ideals 'makes India a valuable partner for the world' (Mohan, 2015, p. 195). Indian democracy should be viewed and studied as a success model. India has also encouraged the introduction and implementation of democratic practices in international organizations. Many theorists like M. Gomichon and S.W. Lee express the view that democracy can only be expressed as a soft power if it has a credible support of hard power. This is mostly because 'powerful actors tend to ignore options that are not congruent with their interests' (Nayar & Paul, 2013, p. 155). India still maintains its legacy of being a successful democracy without the use of coercion and military. The democratic credentials of India are underutilised as a soft power.

It should be realized that engagements with art and culture facilitates a good understanding of the morals, ethics and values which are essential to frame solutions to the rising pressure and tensions in day-to-day life. It is thus inferred that an 'early engagement also helps the young find and channelise innate talents and overcome negativity' (R.K., 2017).

India as a responsive country should work with academia, the private sector and government agencies to improve the quality of citizens' lives which would benefit people all around the world (India rises in global innovation ranking, 2019).

The Indian Council for Cultural Relations and Ministry for Human Resources and Development should engage with Indian embassies abroad and foreign embassies in India to initiate more exchange programmes for students and academicians.

Cricket, hockey football and such popular sports offer varied dimensions to diplomacy. It is equally important to include indigenous and local games and sports to promote diplomatic engagements and international ties.

It is evident that in contemporary times 'space and cyberspace both break the historical constraint of domination through control of physical territory' (Kaul, 2016, p. 362). It is thus of utmost priority that a common protocol for safe and secure cyber space and outer space is developed and India with its expertise would be welcomed as a partner in such endeavours by major powers. In such a scenario, India can also guide developing and smaller states in this regard. Indian government should develop its Department of Science and Technology and Department of Space to engage in probes and experiments in this regard.

India has 36 UNESCO world heritage sites, which takes it to a 6th ranking in the index; it is in 13th position for average tourist spending; bagging 22nd spot for international tourist arrivals; and 23rdposition for participation in major international film festivals (McClory, 2019). Tourism under various heads and specializations should be promoted.

The AYUSH Ministry and pioneering Indian chefs in the field could reach out to the global audience through Indian cuisines and cite its significance in maintaining health. When life style diseases are gripping the world, a change of diet plan is necessary. If the state governments and Union government could devise a proposal through deliberation to ensure food safety and food diplomacy, it could work magic for the Indian foreign relations. The Indian embassies across the world could be roped in for introducing Indian cuisines. The Indian government could extend support to authentic Indian restaurants abroad. A new quality standard should be devised with the backing of Indian government dictated by the Ministry of Consumer Affairs, Food and Public Distribution and Ministry of Health & Family Welfare that validates the authenticity of Indian cuisine served by Indian restaurants abroad, or a body like the FSSAI (Food Safety and Standards Authority of India) could be established towards this purpose.

To be better deliverers of soft power, it is necessary that the diaspora is more enlightened in the values, culture, and ideas representing India. Special focus should be given on how the philosophy and literature of India could be transmitted to younger generation of the diaspora community.

Indian languages, and culture could be imparted to the world if centers are established for this. China has ensured that the Confucius Centers established in different parts of the world help sustain an interest in Chinese culture and language. India should try and develop centres with similar parameters. A focus on developing India's multicultural attributes is essential for enhancing the soft power attributes of the country. ICCR should engage not only in setting up centres promoting Hindi language and the associated culture (24 have been set up so far till August 2020), but also encourage research and promotion of the classical languages and other regional languages and associated cultures of India. Like China, India should not focus on a monoculture trajectory to propogate the culture of India. India's diversity projects the acquiescent attitude of India towards cultures, languages, religions and societies. Therefore, more importance should be placed on promoting India as an advocate and custodian of multiculturalism.

Being an influential force in the institutions and organizations of international reputation will have a better standing for India. India should act as a responsible stakeholder in more global platforms and portray itself as a negotiator aiming for global welfare. This aspect of diplomacy could enhance the Indian soft power. Courses encouraging diplomacy and policy analysis and international relations should be promoted with government interventions towards this end. The image of a naysayer and a mediocre negotiator should be no longer a baggage to India while participating in international platforms and forums. As discussed in the earlier chapters, soft power should be engaged to achieve the same.

In soft power, it is to be understood that the country that can attract others by framing better chronicles and anecdotes from its past and present experiences is better equipped in the race for establishing a world order suiting its interests and demands than a country that has better military strength.

References

In Mongolia, Modi tries his hand on the morin khuur. (2015, May 17). Retrieved from India Today: https://www.indiatoday.in/one-year-of-modi/style-statement/story/modi-plays-fiddle-mongolia-morin-khuur-tsakhiagiin-elbegdorj-253312-2015-05-17

Ananth, V. (2015, May 17). The lesser known history of India's Mongolia ties. Retrieved from Mint: https://www.livemint.com/Politics/niSFjFajO6NsL5CNKIttbN/The-lesser-known-history-of-relations-between-India-and-mode.html

Bahl, A. (2019, January 6). Polo's Forgotten Matriarchs. The Sunday Magazine, The Hindu, p. 7.

Boyd, J. (2021, July 1). The Most Followed Accounts on Twitter. Retrieved from Brandwatch: https://www.brandwatch.com/blog/most-twitter-followers/

Chandavarkar, A. (1972). Technical Cooperation with the Third World. Finance and Development, 17-22.

Chandra, L. (2016, May). India and Mongolia - Shared Heritage. Retrieved from eSamskriti: https://www.esamskriti.com/e/History/Indian-Influence-Abroad/India-And-Mongolia-~-Shared-Heritage-1.aspx

Culture, M. o. (2020, July 9). First five re-printed volumes of Mongolian Kanjur Manuscripts released. Retrieved from Press Information Bureau: https://pib.gov.in/PressReleasePage.aspx?PRID=1637551

Daniyal, S. (2015, May 17). Some tales Modi could tell the Mongols: From Changezi chicken to Bollywood romances. Retrieved from Scroll.In: https://scroll.in/article/727784/some-tales-modi-could-tell-the-mongols-from-changezi-chicken-to-bollywood-romances

Dasgupta, S. (2019, September 18). The civilizational dimension of foreign policy. Retrieved from The Telegraph Online: https://www.telegraphindia.com/opinion/soft-power-linkages-between-india-and-mongolia-the-civilizational-dimension-of-foreign-policy/cid/1705906

EEC. (n.d.). About EEC. Retrieved from EASTERN ECONOMIC FORUM: https://forumvostok.ru/en/about-the-forum/

Enkhsaikhan, J. (2014, April 2). Mongolian foreign policy: a small state with big aspirations. Retrieved from East Asia Forum: https://www.eastasiaforum.org/2014/04/02/mongolian-foreign-policy-a-small-state-with-big-aspirations/

Express, T. I. (2019, September 24). Explained: How India is helping Mongolia's space flight dreams. Retrieved from The Indian Express: https://indianexpress.com/article/explained/india-mongolia-relations-space-flight-6021812/

Huntre! Equine. (n.d.). Retrieved January 11, 2019, from Huntre! Equine: http://huntre.org/AboutHuntre.html

India rises in global innovation ranking. (2019, July 24). The Hindu, p. 13.

India's Strong Economy Continues to Lead Global Growth. (2018, August 8). Retrieved December 21, 2018, from International Monetary Fund: https://www.imf.org/en/News/Articles/2018/08/07/NA080818-India-Strong-Economy-Continues-to-Lead-Global-Growth

ISA. (n.d.). About ISA. Retrieved from International Solar Alliance: https://isolaralliance.org/about/background

Kaul, R. (2016). A Perspective on Space Security. In N. Goswami, India's approach to Asia; Strategy, Geopolitics and Responsibility (pp. 362-371). New Delhi: Pentagon Press.

Khanna, V. (2014, August 18). Cuisine and Diplomacy. Retrieved December 30, 2016, from Public Diplomacy, Ministry of External Affairs: https://mea.gov.in/in-focus-article.htm?23938/Cuisine+and+Diplomacy

Koshy, J. (2019, October 9). India to work with China, Pakistan to gauge impact of climate change. The Hindu, p. 7.

McClory, J. (2019). The Sleeping Giant: India's Soft Power Potential. India Foundation Journal, 11-14.

MET. (n.d.). Vajrapani, the Thunderbolt-bearing Bodhisattva. Retrieved from MET: https://www.metmuseum.org/art/collection/search/38559

Mistry, D. (1998). India's Emerging Space Programme. Pacific Affairs Vol 71, No.2, 151-174.

Mohan, C. R. (2015). Modi's World; Expanding India's Sphere of Influence. New Delhi: Harper Collins.

Nayar, B. R., & Paul, T. (2013). Major-Power Status in the Modern World: India in Comparative Perspective. In K. P. Bajpai, & H. V. Pant, India's Foreign Policy : A Reader; A Critical Issues in Indian Politics (pp. 125-164). New Delhi: Oxford.

Nayar, B. R., & Paul, T. V. (2013). Major Power Status in the Modern World. In K. P. Bajpai, & H. V. Pant, India's Foreign Policy- A Reader; Critical issues in Indian Politics (pp. 126-164). Cambridge: Cambridge University Press.

Nyamdavaa, O. (2015). Ancient Cultural, Ethnic And Religious Ties Between Mongolia And India. World Affairs: The Journal of International Issues , Vol. 19, No. 4 (WINTER, OCTOBER-DECEMBER) , 150-159.

Nye, J. S. (2004). The Means to Sucess in World Politics. New York : Public Affairs.

Parameswaran, P. (2016, April 28). India, Mongolia Launch Military Exercise With Counterterrorism Focus. Retrieved from The Diplomat: https://thediplomat.com/2016/04/india-mongolia-launch-military-exercise-with-counterterrorism-focus/

PMO. (2015, May 17). @narendramodi. Retrieved from Twitter: https://twitter.com/PMOIndia/status/599816661613432832

PMO. (2019, September 2019). @narendramodi. Retrieved from Twitter: https://twitter.com/narendramodi/status/1169492136699600897?lang=en

R.K., U. (2017). Mission Culture; How Ananda Shankar Jayant Thinks Big for Bharat. Retrieved September 7, 2019, from Creative India; Bharat and Beyond: http://creativeindiamag.com/topic/performing-arts/mission-culture-how-ananda-shankar-jayant-thinks-big-for-bharat/

Report, M. (2013, June 19). India-Mongolia Relations. Retrieved from Ministry if External Affairs, Government of India: https://mea.gov.in/Portal/ForeignRelation/India-Mongolia_Relations.pdf

Report, M. (2020, January). Brief on India-Mongolia Bilateral Relations. Retrieved from Ministry of External Affairs: https://www.mea.gov.in/Portal/ForeignRelation/India_Mongolia_2020.pdf

Report, M. (2021, Fecruary). Brief on India-Mongolia Bilateral Relations. Retrieved from Ministry of External Affairs: https://eoi.gov.in/ulaanbaatar/?pdf4346?000

SCO. (n.d.). About SCO. Retrieved from The Shanghai Cooperation Organisation: http://eng.sectsco.org/about_sco/

Soni, S. K. (2016). Emerging Dimensions of India-Mongolia Relations. Indian Foreign Affairs Journal Vol. 11, No. 1 January–March, 51-62.

Stobdan, P. (2015, May 16). In Modi's Mongolia Pivot, a Test of Indian Soft Power. Retrieved from The Wire: https://thewire.in/diplomacy/in-modis-mongolia-pivot-a-test-of-indian-soft-power

Studio.M. (2016, November 2). State-worshipped mountains of Mongolia. Retrieved from Montsame: https://www.montsame.mn/en/read/111331

Tale, T. T. (n.d.). 40 Short Bed Time Panchatantra Stories You must Read To Your 3-10 Year Olds. Retrieved from Tell A Tale: https://www.tell-a-tale.com/10-short-panchatantra-stories-must-read-4-6-year-old-kids/

Thussu, D. K. (2019). Communicating India's Soft Power. India Foundation Journal, 15-17.

Trigunayat, A. A. (2019, September 23). India-Mongolia: The spiritual neighbours embark on an enhancing journey. Retrieved from The Financial Express: https://www.financialexpress.com/defence/india-mongolia-the-spiritual-neighbours-embark-on-an-enhancing-journey/1715139/

Turbat, B. A. (2020, July 30). Science Diplomacy for Enhancing India and Mongolia Bilateral Relations. Retrieved from Artsakh Electronic Library: https://artsakhlib.am/wp-content/uploads/2020/07/Bat-Amgalan-Turbat-Science-Diplomacy-for-Enhancing-India-and-Mongolia-Bilateral-Relations.pdf

Wangchuk, R. N. (2018, April 26). When The World Stood Aside, Mongolia Backed India In Recognising Bangladesh! Retrieved from The Better India: https://www.thebetterindia.com/139407/mongolia-india-bangladesh-united-nations-1971-war/

8. India-Tajikistan Relations: From Civilizational Friends to Strategic Partners

Narendra Sharma[1]

Abstract

Tajikistan and India relations are shaped by shared history, culture and civilizational links, and in modern times, these ties are driven by convergence of geo-political concerns and interests. Taliban takeover of Afghanistan changed the threat perceptions and frequent diplomatic visits between the two countries resulted in closer defence cooperation. But the lack of direct overland connectivity has proved a major hindrance, especially in economic and trade relations. Both sides are committed to exploring alternative routes to increase economic activities. Indian entry to Shanghai Cooperation Organisation (SCO) and challenges like rising radicalization, state-sponsored terrorism, foreign troops withdrawal from Afghanistan and possible return of Taliban have given impetus to cooperation in the realms of security, defence, trade and diplomacy. Proactive diplomacy on both sides is the need of the hour to address the vital issues of connectivity, ensuring stability, security and peace in the region along with economic prosperity via human resource development, shared knowledge and innovation. This paper attempts to analyse the Indo-Tajik relations, alternative routes of connectivity and potential areas of cooperation and as how both Tajikistan and India recognize the centrality of each other in forging a long-term partnership as far as defence and security cooperation is concerned.

Keywords: India, Geo-politics, Tajikistan, Terrorism, SCO, Strategic Partnership

Introduction

Tajikistan and India are two close neighbours who have shared historical, cultural

1 Narendra Sharma is a PhD Scholar with School of Inner Asian Studies, Jawaharlal Nehru University, New Delhi

and civilizational links through history. In modern times, these ties are driven by convergence of geo-political concerns and interests. The increasing threats of separatism, cross-border terrorism and religious extremism have led to greater security and strategic cooperation between the two countries. Taliban takeover of Afghanistan changed the threat perceptions and frequent diplomatic visits between the two countries resulted in closer defence cooperation.

Tajikistan-India bilateral diplomatic ties were established in 1992. Tajik President's state visits in 1995, 2001 and 2006 led to the establishment of development partnership and mutual understanding on security and stability of the region. Each visit shaped bilateral ties in some new dimensions. Indian Prime Minister's visit in 2003 laid down the framework for mutual geo-strategic cooperation in the region while Tajik President's visit in 2012 elevated bilateral partnership to the level of long-term strategic partnership. Capitalizing on this mutual trust, confidence and goodwill, Indian Prime Minister, Narendra Modi's visit to Tajikistan in 2015 built deeper development partnerships between the two countries. . During Tajik president's visit in 2016, India regarded Tajikistan as a major mainstay against the forces of terrorism and extremism and Tajikistan recognizes Indian participation imperative for the security, stability and development of the entire region. Visible results of these diplomatic visits are the establishment of Joint Working Group on Terrorism, Defence and India-Tajikistan Joint Commission for Economic, Scientific and Technological Cooperation along with several business forums, which were instrumental in taking bilateral ties forward in the fields of security, defence and trade spheres. Military hospital at Farkhor, upgradation of Ayni airbase and Varzob-1 hydropower plant, fruit processing plant and IT Centre of Excellence in Dushanbe and other several humanitarian aid and development grants with training and scholarship to Tajik students and defence personnel under ITEC and ICCR are some features of this development partnership. Bilateral relation between Tajikistan and India in diplomatic, defence and security spheres have progressed well but has not developed to its full potential.

Tajikistan is the nearest Central Asian republic to India but due to lack of direct land connectivity, ties of two countries especially in the spheres of trade and economic cooperation are still lagging behind. In this context, it is vital for both countries to seek alternative routes like North-South Transport Corridor and also at the same time seek access to Afghanistan-Pakistan Trade Transit Agreement and UN convention on landlocked countries to seek transit of goods between two countries. Diplomatic efforts have yielded results in enhancing India's geo-political profile in Central Asia and Tajikistan and defence and security cooperation is an important part of this. With new challenges like rising radicalization, drug trafficking and deteriorating situation in Afghanistan and developments like Indian entry to SCO, it necessitates closer partnership in defence and security arenas. This period also becomes important with rising dominance of China in the region and its support to Pakistan. India needs to engage with Russia to reach a consensus for getting a foreign airbase at Ayni that could be a significant step. This study shows how both countries recognize the centrality of each other in forging a long-term strategy to combat cross border terrorism, Islamic radicalization, separatism and securing their national and economic interests.

This article delves deep into the civilizational, cultural, diplomatic, trade, defence and strategic cooperation between two countries and examines how shared cultural history in the past and mutual concerns related to security in present is driving two nations closer.

Historical and Cultural Relations

In the past, Tajikistan and India have enjoyed shared cultural, civilizational and trade relations. Linguistically and culturally, we belong to the same family. Further the similarities between the cultural traditions of Central Asian and Indian people under Avestan and Vedic period only points to our shared historical and cultural relations. Tajik President's own chronicle, "Tajikistan in the mirror of history-from Aryan to Samanids" recalls the old relationship between the people of two countries and points to common Aryan ancestry. Some of the examples of these cultural relations are the adoption of the game of chess and popularity of Indian literary heritage "Panchtamtra" in the Central Asian region (Gulshan, 2015). It is interesting to note that these civilizational links date back to even pre-historic times. Recent research and archaeological excavations clearly show the similar agricultural practices, town planning and regular contact between Indus Valley and Central Asian people. These civilizational links between lands of Amu Darya and Ganga got further strengthened when Bactria, Sogd and Parthia came under a common state along with Gandhara and North-Western India during the period of Achaemenid, Indo- Greek and Kushan empires. Kushan Empire marked the highest level of Cultural exchanges that resulted in the infusion of Indian culture, traditions and Buddhism to the Central Asian region. It was during this time of history that the Great Silk Road served as a medium of exchange of goods, services and ideas rendering peace and prosperity to the people of the region. To sum up, Professor K. Warikoo (2016) states that, "Geographical proximity, ethno linguistic affinity and shared history have formed the basis of a special relationship between India and Tajikistan". This bilateral engagement between the people continued during Turkish and Persian empires that strengthened ties further. There were continuous exchanges of leaders, people, poets, Sufi saints and intellectuals between seats of learning like Samarkand, Bukhara and Delhi. Tajik and Indian poets and scholars made equal contributions to the advancement of Indo-Persian literature in the Indian subcontinent. The popularity of Rabindranath Tagore's poetry in Tajikistan and Bedil's poetry in India and the Indian Prime Minister presenting a miniature painting of Abdul Qadir Bedil to Tajik President points towards shared spiritual and cultural heritage (Olimov, 2016). Mughals who came from this region made Indian their new home but given their emotional and psychological connections with their homeland, they continued their engagements with the region in one or the other form. According to Richard Foltz, this two hundred years of continuous engagement with the Central Asian region and especially influence of Tajik nobility (who belonged to the same Indo-Aryan Brach of Aryans of which one part settled in North and North-West India) in Mughal courts led to the development of India's cosmopolitan culture. It would be naive to assume that this engagement was just one way, but traveling of Buddhism , traditional knowledge of medicine and herbs and India traders, poets and monks to this region only points that our shared past experienced mutual influence. Now, with India and Central Asia coming under the Russian and British empires respectively and later on rivalry and mutual suspicion between the two empires widened the distance between two regions of shared close cultural and historical relations. As Professor K. Warikoo (2016) points out that, "This Russian policy of strategic diversion was countered by the British by adopting a sustained forward policy in the region". By the treaty of 1907, both Tsarist Russia and British decided that Wakhan Corridor, a narrow strip of Afghan territory, would be separating Russian Central Asian territories and British Indian possessions and rendering a serious long-term blow to the connectivity between the two regions. Thus is it clear that this Great Game' rivalry between two empires put a stoppage to the centuries old civilizational links between the two regions. Tajik people and poets like Mirzo Tursun-Zoda supported Indian freedom movement. Indian independence resulted in the forming of two separate states namely India and Pakistan proved catastrophic to the age-old connections with the Central Asian region as direct land connectivity to the wider South Asian region was lost. And again during the Soviet era, there was commonality of interests and close cooperation in science, politics, economics and culture. Tajik Soviet Socialist Republic enjoyed close trade and cultural relations with India. These relations were regulated through Moscow and the extent and intensity of these relations were still limited. However, with the signing of Indo-Soviet Friendship Treaty in 1971, cultural exchanges between India and Central Asian republics increased considerably (Singh, 2003). During this period of time, Hindi films enjoyed much popularity in Central Asia. During Cold War era, India despite being the founding member of Non-alignment moment remained a close ally of Soviet Union and for that matter Central Asian republics. Friendly Indo-Soviet ties were instrumental in forging deeper Indian contacts with Central Asia in comparison to other southern neighbours and this very good mutual understanding along with age old brotherly bonding and commonality of interest and views in modern times provided India an added advantage to establish political relations with newly emerged Central Asian republics after the disintegration of Soviet Union.

Soviet disintegration resulted in the emergence of five Central Asian Republics namely Kazakhstan, Kyrgyzstan, Tajikistan, Turkmenistan and Uzbekistan in the 1990s. India was one of the first countries to recognize their Independence and started to establish diplomatic relations with newly emerged republics by segregating its overall Soviet-era ties by Republic wise. The sudden break up of Soviet Union brought socio-economic miseries to these republics and these miseries coupled with the transitional pain resulted in widespread poverty, unemployment and political instability in many countries. These countries started to interact with regional and global powers to overcome this situation. During this time, India was in shock due to break up of its dependable ally and political and economic instability at home further delayed Indian outreach to the region. However India was quick to realize this delay and now it has a strategic partnership with three of the five Central Asian republics and trade is also picking up, though slowly. Indian measures like 'Connect Central Asia' policy, and also holding an India-Central Asia Dialogue at Track II annually in one of the republics have contributed to the closer ties (Singh, 2003). Though India and Central Asian countries enjoy friendly relationship, the economic and trade engagement between the two sides has been much below its potential. The countries of Central Asia are rich in hydrocarbons, mineral and other natural resources and are close to India geographically. Geographically, the strategic location of these countries also makes them a bridge between different regions of Asia and between Europe and Asia. Although the significance of the region in India's economic and energy security is clear, lack of direct surface connectivity has been affecting the economic engagement. However, the recent progress in North-South Transport Corridor will certainly improve the connectivity between the two regions.

Geographically, Tajikistan is nearest to India and given its geo-strategic position, it is important not only to India but also regional and global actors as well. Further, Tajikistan is rich in mineral and natural resources and it has a fast-growing consumer market and India is important to it due to its status as an emerging economic and political power in the world. Mutual interests of both sides rest primarily on economic and trade cooperation, regional security and stability and maintaining of strategic order. As far as this modern relationship between two countries is concerned, it is simply not based on close civilizational, cultural and trade ties but both sides find several commonalities. In the present time, the similarity of worldviews, common threat concerns like cross-border terrorism, religious extremism and separatism, high level of mutual confidence and trust, their commitment to build modern secular, pluralist and democratic polity, securing stability and peace in Afghanistan, promoting social-ethno-linguistic and cultural harmony, adherence to non-interference and peaceful co-existence and promoting overall trade, cultural and technological cooperation are imparting new colors to the dynamic partnership between two countries. Tajikistan provides a special place to India in its foreign policy due to its close geographical proximity and age-old close historical, cultural and trade ties and mutual concerns related to regional security and stability. Referring to these bilateral relations between two countries, Tajik President stressed: "the Republic of Tajikistan within the framework of its bilateral and multilateral relations with India is looking at it as a factor for peace and stability in the region". The disintegration of USSR followed by Tajik civil war disrupted Tajikistan-India relations for some time. But it also gave an opportunity to engage with new sovereign Tajik state. Attempts by outside powers to secure geo-political and economic interests (New Great Game) coupled by rising threats of cross-border terrorism; extremism and volatile Afghanistan situation have turned Tajikistan a high priority in India's foreign policy, which led to high-level diplomatic exchanges between the two countries.

Diplomatic and Economic Cooperation

Formal diplomatic ties were established between the two countries on 28 August, 1992. Since then, Indo-Tajik cooperation has covered a broad spectrum of fields from diplomatic, economic, cultural, defence and security to education, human resource development, science and technology, academic and humanitarian arenas. Diplomatic visits by leaders from both sides have helped in strengthening bilateral ties in these spheres and thus taking bilateral cooperation to new heights. Tajik President has visited India several times so far. It was during the first state visit of Tajik President in 1995 when a mutual understanding was reached on Afghanistan for security and stability of the region (MEA, 2017). However, the Taliban took over Afghanistan and escalation of cross-border terrorism in the Indian state of Jammu and Kashmir started a new phase in the bilateral cooperation between two countries. Here it is also important to note that Pakistani sponsored extremism and terrorism in Afghanistan had a direct spill over effect on Tajikistan and thus worsened its internal security scenario. Now worried about their respective internal security and stability, both countries cooperated well in supporting Northern Alliance led by Tajik leadership of Ahmad Shah Masood against the Taliban. Against these developments, landmark visits by Tajik President in 1999 and 2001 and Indian Prime Minister in 2003 concretized the ties in geo-political and security realms in the wake of rising threats of state sponsored terrorism and religious extremism and Indian Prime Minister Vajpayee described this joint Tajik-Indian action as a "stabilizing factor" for the region (MEA, 2018). It was due to these diplomatic efforts that India was able to garner Tajik support for Indian claim of permanent membership at United Nations Security Council and entry to Shanghai

Cooperation Organization (SCO). At the same time Tajikistan found a reliable partner in its pursuit of regional security and stability and economic development of the country.

Although each visit brought both countries closer but due to political instability at home which resulted in political indecisiveness in foreign affairs and lack of political and bureaucratic will to implement the already signed mutual agreements failed to raise India's geo-political and strategic profile in the Central Asian region. However, developments like Kargil war and persistent volatile security situation in the neighbourhood provided a new urgency to the bilateral cooperation especially in the fields of security and defence. The visit of Indian defence Minister in 2002 points to this urgency and growing defence cooperation between two countries. The military hospital at Farkhor and Ayni air base for infant Tajik air force are physical signs of this new cooperation.

Indian President Pratibha Patil's visit enhanced goodwill, trust and mutual confidence between the two countries. During the state visit of Tajik President in 2012, both sides decided to elevate their bilateral relations to the level of a long-term strategic partnership. Indian Prime Minister's visit in 2015 provided further impetus to these relations. On his last stoppage to Tajikistan, Narendra Modi remarked: "This is the last stop on my visit to the five Central Asian countries. But, we sometimes save the special one for the last". He pointed out to closest linguistic, civilizational and historical links with Tajikistan. Tajik President's visit to India in 2016 reinforced the commitment of both countries to take bilateral ties to a new level by improving overall bilateral security cooperation, capacity building, and information exchanges and via active coordination at regional and multilateral platforms. India regarded Tajikistan's role as a 'mainstay' against forces of extremism, religious radicalization, and terrorism (MEA, 2015). These diplomatic visits also resulted in the strengthening of cooperation between two countries in areas like human resource development by providing increased number of scholarships and training to Tajik students via ITEC in areas ranging from English language, banking, and finance, IT to industrial development and management and defence training and identifying new areas of cooperation like tourism, agriculture and space. Tajikistan attracts the largest share of humanitarian and development assistance in the form if aids and material support and it has significantly build the IT capacity of Tajikistan while at the same time enhancing Indian strategic outreach in the region (Gulshan, 2015).

Diplomatic ties shaped by regular visits of leaders, bureaucrats and other cultural and academic missions resulted in the signing of several mutual agreements and MOUs including those of economic and trade nature and helped in strengthening defence, security and strategic cooperation, but the lack of direct overland connectivity hindered trade cooperation. Though economic and trade ties between Tajikistan and India go back to Silk Road days, in present times it's a low-key affair due to structural and connectivity hurdles. There is a vast potential of trade between resource rich Tajikistan and technology-rich India. Private sector cooperation is an important aspect of trade relations that can increase the competitive nature of Tajikistan's manufacturing units thus leading to Tajikistan's export diversification and economic independence in the wake of dominating cheap Chinese goods. In return India can avail the benefit of the vast potential of hydro power in Tajikistan for its energy security. The areas of cooperation between two countries are like pharmaceuticals, education, health, energy, tele-communication, and infrastructure.

Structural changes in the trade relations between two countries are the need of the hour. The reasons for this low level of trade between the two countries are of direct overland connectivity due to political differences between India and Pakistan, expensive and unreliable Mumbai- Bandar Abbas- Dushanbe route, macroeconomic instability in Central Asia inadequate banking facilities, strict visa regimes, language barriers and absence of direct and daily air connectivity are some of them (Warikoo, 2015).

Indian access to Afghanistan-Pakistan Trade Transit Agreement can tap the vast potentiality of trade between India and Central Asia. And, further establishment of India-Pakistan- Afghanistan-Central Asia Transport Corridor will reduce the cost of transportation significantly (Warikoo, 2016). Political relations need to be improved between India and Pakistan and political stability in Afghanistan is the need of the hour. However, Indian hopes lie mainly on the North-South Transport Corridor and recent progress in this project is a positive sign. According to the respective embassy websites, both countries have a Joint Inter- governmental commission led by the ministry of economy and trade that reviews the existing level of cooperation in several fields. Apart from this, several major agreements and bilateral treaties like Agreement for Bilateral Investment Protection, Air Services Agreement and Agreement on Long-term Cooperation in Trade, Economic and Industry and institutional arrangements like setting up of an Indo-Tajik Joint Commission for Economic, Scientific and Technological Cooperation and business forums and even after their several rounds of meetings have strengthened bilateral trade while at the same time identifying the new areas of cooperation. A number of civilian projects like the reconstruction of the Varzob-1 hydro power plant, Fruit Processing Plant and IT Centre in Dushanbe have strengthened the existing relations between two countries. Indian Prime Minister's visit to Tajikistan in 2015, where he addressed an agricultural workshop, points to the vast potential of cooperation in farming techniques, equipment and space technology (MEA, 2015).

Defence and Strategic Cooperation

One of the vibrant dimensions of these ever growing bilateral ties is the increasing cooperation in security and defence related fields between the two countries. Mutual interests concerning peace, security and stability of Central Asia in the wake of volatile Afghan situation coupled with rising threats of religious extremism and cross-border terrorism brought two countries closer in defence and strategic partnership. These developments increased the diplomatic efforts between two countries for closer defence ties. In this context, Indian Prime Minister's visit in 2003 laid down the framework for mutual geo-strategic cooperation in the region while Tajik President's visit in 2012 elevated bilateral partnership to the level of long-term strategic partnership (MEA, 2012). Today, joint military exercises, defence personnel training, Ayni airbase, military hospital, defence material supplies and Joint Working Group on Terrorism are the hallmark of this partnership. Although, Indian entry to SCO provided it some influence but entry to other regional organizations like 'Dushanbe Four' is still needed to push these ties forward. It is clear that Pakistan has a role in spreading religious extremism and cross-border terrorism that is harming both Tajikistan and India. Pakistan is using this platform to secure a position in the Central Asian region and is denying India's entry to this organization which is a Tajik Initiative to counter narco trade and promoting economic cooperation and sharing electricity. Indian entry into this organization can add greater significance to it (Dutta, 2015). The establishment of Joint Working Group on terrorism, defence and sharing of intelligence and expanding cooperation between heads of relevant organizations are positive signs of our growing security and defence cooperation with the country. During Indian Prime Minister's visit to the country in 2015, both sides expressed satisfaction with growing defence ties and at the same time reaffirmed their commitment for closer cooperation in this field. During Tajik president's visit in 2016, India regarded Tajikistan as a major mainstay against the forces of terrorism and extremism and Tajikistan recognizes Indian participation imperative for the security, stability and development of the entire region (Sharma, 2016).

Tajikistan and India are faced with a wide range of common questions connected with most important challenges such as terrorism, religious extremism and drug trafficking. However, these security challenges to regional peace and stability are not the only reasons of Indian outreach in this region, given fast developing Pakistan-China axis in the region, Indian need to maintain its strategic influence in the region. Stephen Blank (2012) in this regard opines that, "Two key Indian objectives are to deny Pakistan and China, her key rivals and threats, opportunities to increase their strategic capability by gaining predominant influence in Central Asia or by threatening India's assets there. Enhancing Indian influence in the region equates to a strategy of strategic denial". Both Russia and Central Asian states have welcomed Indian role in this region and Central Asian states especially Tajikistan and Uzbekistan recognize India as an important factor in the regional peace and stability in Afghanistan and Central Asian region. Further, India's accession to SCO provides it a legitimate platform to enhance its political and strategic profile in the region. However, India's increasing closeness to the USA may result in the formation of Russia-China-Pakistan axis and may harm its economic and strategic aspirations in the region. Russian cooperation is vital for India's presence in this region and for this India needs to sort out the apprehensions of the long-standing ally in this regard.

Way Forward

In the wake of volatile Afghanistan situation and escalation of cross-border terrorism situation in the Indian state of Jammu and Kashmir in the 1990s, India started defence cooperation with Tajikistan in order to counter state-sponsored terrorism, extremism and separatism. It is the most vibrant aspect of bilateral cooperation between the two countries and has been consistently growing in newer areas. But, just one-way cooperation in defence and security has its own limitations. Tajikistan needs to reciprocate Indian eagerness to become the major security and defence partner of the country by providing it access to use Ayni airbase and other similar projects. Indian and Tajik diplomatic pro-activeness is required to take Russia in confidence to make it a reality. What is important to note here is that similar kind of security situation has arisen in the extended neighbourhood of India. With the new challenge like emergence of new radical Islamist groups like ISIS, rise in cross-border and state sponsored terrorism, withdrawal of foreign troops from Afghanistan and resurgent Taliban, Al-Qaeda and extremist groups coupled with fast changing geo-political global power equations and security environment necessitates deeper defence and security cooperation between Tajikistan, Afghanistan and India. Pakistan is continuing with its old tactics of sponsoring cross-border terrorism to disturb peace and stability in Afghanistan and India. Non-state actors like Haqqani Network and Taliban and other militant groups sponsored by Pakistan are continuously attacking Indian humanitarian and development projects in the region in order to curb growing Indian influence in Afghanistan and Central Asian republics. Apart from India and Afghanistan, countries like Tajikistan, Uzbekistan and Iran are also suffering from the terrorism emanating from Pakistan-based terror camps. India needs to formulate a proper action plan to take these countries on board to united stand against state-sponsored terrorism and diplomatic efforts to isolate Pakistan over this. With the formation of the hostile China-Pakistan axis through China-Pakistan Economic Corridor (CPEC) that violates India's territorial integrity, India needs to pursue a well-coordinated defence and security policy as part of its foreign policy with regional and global powers like Russia and USA. Although in the case of Central Asia and for that matter Tajikistan, India is doing this since the emergence of extremist Taliban and the rise of state-sponsored terrorism in the 1990s. But general observation has been that India has been reluctant to expand its geo-political profile in the Central Asian region and Tajikistan in particular in comparison with regional players like Iran and China. What is worth mentioning in the relationship of two countries is the fact that both are strategic partner to each other and recognize the centrality of each other in maintaining peace and stability in Central and South Asian region. During Tajik president's visit in 2016, India regarded Tajikistan as a major mainstay against the forces of terrorism and extremism and Tajikistan recognizes Indian participation imperative for the security, stability and development of the entire region. Capitalizing on this mutual trust, confidence and goodwill and building deeper development partnerships will certainly bode well for India's broader aspirations in energy-rich Central Asia in general and strategically located Tajikistan in particular.

Conclusion

Emphasis on having close historical, cultural, and civilizational and trade ties between the two countries needs to be matched by significant improvement in economic and trade relations. Proactive diplomacy is the need of the hour to address the vital issues of connectivity, ensuring stability, security and peace in the region along with economic prosperity via human resource development, shared knowledge and innovation. Both countries need to build a long-term strategy and secure their national interests by curbing the menace of separatism, cross-border terrorism and religious extremism. There are immense opportunities and challenges before the two countries, but sustained and close cooperation in diplomatic, trade, defence and security arenas will certainly move the relations between the two countries to new heights. As Bedil, the Tajik poet urged, "The Sea of time and place, for you, is but one gulp limit, not your boundless imagination".

References

Bakshi, Jyotsna (2013), *Geopolitical Dynamism of India-Tajikistan Relations*, Pentagon Press, New Delhi.

Dutta, Mondira (2015), "Tajik-Afghan border: Countering Drug Trafficking for Regional Stability", in Warikoo, K. and Kh. Umarov (eds.) *Tajikistan in the 21st Century, Society, Politics and Economy*, Pentagon Press, New Delhi.

Embassy of India, Dushanbe, Tajikistan (http://indianembassytj.com/)

Embassy of the Republic of Tajikistan in India

Emomali Rahmon (2007), "15 Years of Establishment Tajik-Indian Diplomatic Relations", Diplomatic View, Aug-Sep 2007, p.8-11

Gulshan, Zugurova (2015), "Tajikistan-India Relations since 1991", in Warikoo, K. and Kh. Umarov (eds.) *Tajikistan in the 21st Century, Society, Politics and Economy*, Pentagon Press, New Delhi.

Himalayan Research and Cultural Foundation (http://www.himalayanresearch.org/) Institute for Defense Studies and Analyses (http://www.idsa.in/)

Indian Council of World Affairs (http://www.icwa.in/crtajik.html)

Kundu, Nivedita (2011), "India-Tajikistan bilateral relationship", Russia and India Report, September 2, 2011 (https://in.rbth.com/articles/2011/09/02/india- tajikistan_ bilateral_relationship_12949)

Ministry of External Affairs, Government of India (http://www.mea.gov.in).

Olimov, Muzaffar (2016), "Tajikistan-India Bilateral Relations: Problems and Prospects", Himalayan and Central Asian Studies, Vol. (20): 15-27

Rajabov, Habibullo (2003), "Ten Years of Cultural Relations of Tajikistan and India, India and Tajikistan Revitalizing a Traditional Relationship", Publication of Maulana Abul Kalam Azad Institute Of Asian Studies, New Delhi.

Sharma, Angira Sen (2015), "Dushanbe Four" Initiative and its impact on Regional Cooperation", in Warikoo, K. and Kh. Umarov (eds.) *Tajikistan in the 21st Century, Society, Politics and Economy*, Pentagon Press, New Delhi.

Singh, Mahavir (2003), "India and Tajikistan: Revitalizing a traditional Relationship", Anamika Publishers and Distributors (P) LTD. New Delhi.

Warikoo, K. (2005), *Central Asia: Emerging New Order*, Har-Anand publications, New Delhi.

Warikoo, K. (2007), *Afghanistan: Challenges and Opportunities*, Pentagon Press, New Delhi.

Warikoo, K. and Singh Mahavir (2004), *Central Asia since Independence*, Shipra Publications, New Delhi.

Warikoo, K. and Umarov Kh. (2015), *Tajikistan in the 21st Century, Society, Politics and Economy*, Pentagon Press, New Delhi.

Index

O

P

Q

R

S